Books by Sonia Levitin

REIGNING CATS
AND DOGS

REIGNING

DRAWINGS BY JOAN BERG VICTOR

Sonia Levitin

CATS AND DOGS

Atheneum   1978   NEW YORK

Library of Congress Cataloging in Publication Data

Levitin, Sonia, 1934–
    Reigning cats and dogs.

    1. Dogs—Legends and stories.   2. Cats—Legends and
stories.   3. Levitin, Sonia, 1934–   I. Title.
SF426.2.L48   1978   818'.5'407   77-15811
ISBN 0-689-10868-0

For

LLOYD

with Love

REIGNING CATS
AND DOGS

1

I T M I G H T S E E M S T R A N G E and even heartless
that on the eve of our German shepherd's tenth birthday we decided to get a puppy.

("No, Mother, not to replace the old dog. I'm not
saying he's no good just because he's old. Well, I *hope*
he won't feel rejected.")

My mother was against the whole idea from the
start. She told me so. But the vet gave us at least partial
approval. He shrugged and scratched his chin. "Who
knows? It might give Baron a new interest in life. On
the other hand . . ."

We hoped for the best. Baron had lived with us since he was twelve weeks old. By now our habits were meshed like those of a long and happily wed couple. We had developed an almost telepathic communication. And we loved him. The new puppy was to ease us over the inevitable passage, and in no way to undermine Baron's place in our hearts.

Baron, maybe because he was the first dog Lloyd and I ever owned together, was special. He was Shari's staunch protector from the time she was three. If, in her exuberant play, Shari happened to stomp on his paw, he quietly retreated to a safer spot and still adored her. From the beginning, Dan made Baron his confidant. I would see him crouched before the dog whispering confessions, murmuring of matters too deep for the rest of us. For Lloyd, Baron was the perfect hiking companion; for me, a gentle friend and trustworthy babysitter. Somehow, each of us thought of Baron as his very own dog, and he played his various roles superbly.

As a pup he'd been ridiculously easy to train. It took only three days to housebreak him. Only once did I have to point out that the children's toys were not for chewing, and only once did I have to reprimand him for stealing a plateful of cheese from the kitchen counter. He took criticism seriously and kept his promises.

Aside from the normal decencies, Baron had also

learned a few subtle extras. He could locate a lost baseball in the thorniest thicket. He brought in the newspaper—without teeth marks! He knew how to vocalize
his desire for milk with an operatic "Grr—awhoo—
whoo-whoo." He loved riding in the car and wisely
emptied his bladder before every outing. Yes, having
Baron around was calming, easy—so *effortless*.

But don't get the idea that he was a paragon or a
cream puff. He had his faults. When he felt like chasing
the blue jays, you could scream yourself hoarse; he
simply played deaf. He never could tolerate the milkman, who daily dropped his cartons in sheer terror,
trying desperately to retain some semblance of dignity while Baron lunged at the gate, barking like a
maniac.

Nor was Baron a particularly sociable dog. He
was not popular with the other neighborhood animals.
Once the children gave him a doggie birthday party
with hamburger cake. It was touch and go.

Only once did I know him to attempt a mating. It
was with Squaw, the attractive black Labrador who belonged to our friends around the corner. During one of
our afternoon walks, when Squaw was in heat, Baron
claimed the prerogative of a long-standing friendship
and mounted her with enthusiasm.

She gave him a devastating growl and a snap.
Baron ran home, rebuffed forever.

Shortly thereafter, he lost his head over the pint-size dachshund next door, incongruously named Floyd. That little dog went into heat so often that we were convinced she must be part rabbit. And each time, Baron was sent into such a paroxysm of moans and howls that we finally had to offer him tranquilizers. He never tried to force his attentions on the "dachsey," but eyed her with tenderness as he suffered from afar.

It was not tenderness that made him, during a friendly poker game, suddenly lunge at one of Lloyd's buddies and pin him to the wall. Nor was it meritorious that he once bit a poor goat that was tethered to a tree, nor that he routed a God-fearing missionary out of our cul-de-sac and sent him fleeing across the street and into the back of a dump truck.

No—Baron was not perfect, but we had all made many mutual adjustments over the years, and what could be better proof of love?

All this, now, by way of introduction, to establish our situation as we began the search for a new puppy.

We all agreed that the pup must be a true brother to Baron, a long-haired, black German shepherd, just like our darling, so that the two would match exactly. Our reasoning was simple: we were convinced that all Baron's virtues were inherent in his exact color, size, and breed.

6

Where does one find such a dog? Not in pet shops. They specialize in poodles and Afghan hounds. Certainly not in the want ads, where hybrid pups of uncertain genealogy are touted by the dozens. We decided then and there that Baron must become a father. For a few weeks I propositioned every passing female German shepherd, but to no avail. Their owners sometimes gave me dubious looks—I felt like a pervert.

At last I consulted our vet. Ten-year-old dogs, he told us, are usually infertile. Or impotent. We kept this shocking news from Baron and proceeded to look around for that perfect pup.

Meanwhile, Baron had an encounter with a skunk one night, and the experience nearly did him in. For three days he lay on his side, moaning, refusing to eat, and he was never quite the same afterward. Or perhaps the episode forced us to focus on his physical condition. He was aging rapidly and pathetically. His once-full face had become pinched and drawn, perhaps a result of the chronic pain of arthritis. He moved like a ninety-five-year-old. If he climbed the stairs one day, he paid for it the next. He tried valiantly to be his old sporting self, recalling, perhaps, how he used to run three miles without flagging. Now he could barely make it to the corner.

The vet gave him a year—two at the most.

Now, what was our real motive for seeking a puppy at this particular juncture? We discussed it at length. We agreed that for slobbery sentimentalists like us it would be very hard to face Baron's death without another dog in the house. There was also a very practical reason: we never wanted to be without a watchdog, and it takes a pup about nine months to grow into that responsibility.

We made the mistake that all people make when they plan to get a new pet, or take in a boarder, or have another baby. We never considered that the newcomer would have his own personality, make his own demands, intrude upon our time and our territory.

Oh no—*our* pup would be bought and paid for as an *apprentice*. He would grow quickly, with alert attention to every detail, his only desire being to learn from his older "brother" how to protect and defend the homestead. He would follow Baron's every movement, seeking only to emulate him and thereby to please us. In time—very gradually, of course—he would also win a measure of our affection. Of love we thought not one whit. We thought only of duplicating Baron.

We got, instead, Barney.

2

W E H A V E A N old-fashioned grocery store in town where people tack ads to the bulletin board. Someone had advertised on a three-by-five card GERMAN SHEP-HERD PUPS. AKC REGISTERED. SHOW QUALITY.

I tore off the card, rushed home and telephoned. The young woman told me that her prize-winning German shepherd had sired a litter for her friend who owned a kennel near Pomona, some sixty miles away. She advised me to phone the kennel immediately. Yes, they did have some long-hair pups just about ready to be weaned.

That night I delivered the news to my family. "They have three long-hair shepherds at the kennel. The reason dogs like Baron are so hard to find—they're called 'coated' dogs—" I said smugly, "is that they're not used in shows. Breeders are trying to breed them out. The long coat is from a recessive gene."

They gazed at me, amazed at my wisdom. Lloyd asked, "Are the coated dogs cheaper?"

"No. The same. One hundred and fifty dollars. With papers." Oh, I was proud of what I'd accomplished all in a day.

We began, like prospective parents, to talk about "our" puppy in terms that already settled the issue.

If Dan had been home (he was away at college), no doubt everything would have been different. Dan is the scholar among us—cautious, deliberative, sensible and thorough. Dan would have asked certain questions, like, shouldn't we check with the vet? Should we, perhaps, compare these with puppies from another kennel? Isn't Pomona a heck of a long way to go for a puppy?

But Danny, bless him, was away at M.I.T., where his good sense had landed him, and we—we three sat there at the kitchen table and readily decided that our puppy waited for us at that kennel in Pomona, and that we had to fetch him at the earliest possible moment —next Saturday.

During the week I telephoned (long distance) almost daily to question the kennel-lady. I've always known that much can be gained by asking questions. It helps if they're the *right* questions. What did the puppies look like? "Cute," she said. "And one in particular loves water. Yessir, plays in his water pail all day. Cute."

Did she think a new puppy would get along with the old dog?

"Well, dear heart," she said, "he'll probably be grateful for the company. The pup might arouse his fatherly instincts."

I could hardly wait until Saturday.

We told Shari she could bring along a friend. Thirteen-year-olds always bring along a friend, no matter what the occasion.

We left early. Our puppy had to be home by lunchtime. He must not begin his life with us by missing a meal. Lloyd was adamant about that. (I've noticed that people impute to others—even animals—their own values.)

So, although we usually sleep late on Saturdays, on this particular morning we were up and on the freeway by eight-thirty. In the back seat, the girls giggled softly, anticipating the delights of the day.

We arrived at the kennel, a ramshackle old house

and broken-down yard sprouting an acre of weeds and junk. The house sagged like an Alfred Hitchcock backdrop. I guess I'd expected something—well, something more *official*-looking.

As we rolled into the driveway, some two dozen caged dogs commenced the most awful racket I'd ever heard. Their rage, their frantic howling, seemed all out of proportion with the mere fact of our arrival. I had a queer feeling that they were heralding some other catastrophe.

The lady came out. Not *the* kennel-lady—she was "up north for a dog show." This was the kennel-lady's helper, a laconic, sulky-looking woman dressed for a part in *The Grapes of Wrath*.

I could see immediately that she was a realist. By neither sign nor word did she try to silence the howling dogs. Instead, she walked over to a small wire enclosure where several puppies frantically wriggled and leaped, their little squeals of excitement all but drowned out by the racket of their elders.

Lloyd hollered above the din: "We came to see the males!"

The lady thrust in her hand and, miraculously, from amid that roiling, whirling mass of fur, plucked out one of the puppies. "This here's it. The male."

The other dogs had stopped barking. Some were

pacing like restless wolves, while others stood trans-
fixed in their cages, watching.

"Only one male?" I said weakly. "I thought we'd
have a choice."

"Had two males and a female. Female's spoken for.
Other male was bought yesterday."

So, this was it—our pup.

Did we look at each other questioningly? Did we
perchance inquire about future litters? Did we even
try to negotiate the price because of the fact that we
were offered no real choice?

Did we ask to inspect the dam? Did we demand
to examine the lineage? Did we examine the pup
thoroughly, to judge by teeth and coat and attitude
whether he be the hearty, healthy, intelligent, playful
but earnest companion we desired?

I knelt down and felt the puppy all over, realizing
it was my duty as the mother of the family to do something that at least seemed authoritative. (Oh, I wished
then I'd read that book—the one that tells how to examine a new puppy, how to grade him for such traits
as dominance, sociability, trainability, how to employ
simple, reasonable little tests to determine whether this
is the dog for you. It would have felt so good to appear
knowledgeable in front of that kennel-lady's helper.)
But even as I prodded the puppy I knew that she knew

it was only for show. I thought to give her a stern, skeptical glance. I'd be darned if I'd let that lady think I was going to take the first puppy she threw at us!

"He's pretty thin," I ventured at last.

"Oh, we keep 'em thin. Healthier. Keeps 'em from gettin' hip problems later. Dysplasia."

I nodded thoughtfully. "I see. Yes, our dog has always had a hip problem. Guess he was allowed to get too fat as a pup." My voice had taken on the same twang as that of the kennel-lady's helper. I am a weak person. Weak.

"Yeah. Must be. This 'ere pup's fully weaned. Lively."

The puppy was, in fact, spinning like a top.

Lloyd knelt down and gave him a pat.

Shari, all smiles, knew no other word but *cute*. Her friend, braces and all, could not outsmile Shari, but added the word *adorable*.

I turned to Lloyd, stalling. "He's not *all* black, is he?"

"Nice markings," said the lady.

Lloyd said, "We'd better get going. It's a long drive. Lunchtime."

With that, he picked up the puppy, tucked it under his arm, and headed for the car, motioning that I was to go through the ramshackle door to write out a check

14

and collect feeding instructions. And that's what I did.

Dazed, I handed the lady my check and it was all over. We were rolling out of the driveway with our small animal settled in Shari's lap, purring—yes, purring—and grunting like a baby rooting around for mamma.

As we turned out onto the road, I saw another woman emerge from the old house. They stood there talking, and their smiles and waves struck me as rather conspiratorial. But I sublimated the thought and glanced around at our puppy, the baby.

I took in the camel-colored paws, so comically huge. I saw the full, silky ruff of black, gold, and tan. I gazed at his large, pointed ears, his liquid round eyes, and his tail, which even then was outrageously long and bushy, as if it had been stolen from a fox or a squirrel and hastily attached to him. That tail . . .

With a strange lump in my throat I said, "Here, let me hold him. You girls are too rough."

"But, Mother!"

Fiercely I reiterated that only my arms were tender enough for this very expensive "investment" we'd made. And so I held him, his soft head resting under my chin, and I felt those very same mother-stirrings I'd known before (and would, heaven help me, soon know again), and I asked, "What shall we name him?"

We bandied about a few names—Brutus, Mitch, Teddy, Foxy, Fonzie. Then Shari came out with it. Barney. And immediately we knew. A name isn't really *given*. It comes and thrusts itself upon you, zinging down like an arrow from somewhere in space, and you know it's right. It sinks and sticks. It fits.

Thus, after we'd had him for only about five minutes, we already called him Barney.

3

L E T M E M A K E this perfectly clear: we are acquainted with Pavlov's dogs no less than with Lassie. Sure, we harbor a certain nutty romanticism about dogs, but we know that a dog, like a person, needs not only abundant love but proper training and firm discipline.

You see, we were armed with sound psychological insights as we entered into this new relationship with Barney. First, the pup had to have his own bed. Lloyd said so. Not just a mat on the floor in the garage, like Baron used, but a bona-fide bed with a padded cushion.

Lloyd parked in front of Newberry's. While I was buying the doggie bed I was also supposed to rustle up five or six cardboard cartons. What for? Why, to make a little enclosure to keep the puppy from roaming around the garage at night.

I made a big mistake. I laughed. Lloyd got that look on his face. There are certain things he *knows* about animals. Submissively, I got the bed, the cushion, and the cartons.

Once home, we allowed Barney to sniff around the patio. We fed him milk and cottage cheese. We admired him. The neighbors came over to praise our puppy and congratulate us on our choice. "Oh, see how he follows Lloyd," they said. "See how he already knows his master."

Lloyd beamed as the puppy scampered after him, sniffing at his new thirty-five-dollar Wallabees.

We did not let the neighbors stay very long: we didn't want to overstimulate our new baby. We walked them to the gate, and oh! our wonderful puppy did not even try to run out. No, he stayed right by his master's foot, hovering over the thirty-five-dollar Wallabee, and just as the final neighborly farewell was uttered, Lloyd yelped. The pup jumped. We all cast our eyes upon the shoe. Simultaneously we grasped the situation, and nobody laughed—not yet—as the wet spot slowly seeped into the soft leather.

Lloyd gazed up at us, unruffled. "This dog," he said, "obviously does not respect me."

We all howled with laughter. The puppy ran around in delighted circles, like a kid pulling monkey-shines when the boss comes to dinner. Right then and there, I think, his toilet training was set back by about four months.

After a hasty consultation we decided to ignore the puppy's breach of etiquette and initiate Phase Two, The Meeting. As the kennel-lady had explicitly instructed, I carried Barney downstairs and out into the backyard to meet Baron. I felt as if I were about to offer him up on some ritual altar.

"Look, Baron!" I called out, mimicking the cheeriness of Mary Poppins. "Look what I've brought you! A puppy! It's yours!"

Baron believed me. Looking like one of those animated pictures of a brontosaurus rex, he lumbered over, fully expecting to eat his puppy for lunch.

I knelt down, with Barney still in my lap. Suddenly the puppy—that nineteen-pound fireball—shrank. He not only shrank, he apparently passed out.

Baron assiduously began to sniff, going over every inch of the puppy from nose to tail and back again, while Barney lay limp in abject surrender, his attitude signifying clearly: "Forget about me, buster, I'm already dead."

Satisfied that the newcomer posed no clear and present competition, Baron stalked off, plunked himself down on the lawn, and nonchalantly proceeded to scratch a nonexistent flea behind his ear. He let us know that the whole affair meant nothing to him. Nothing.

I set Barney down. With Baron at a distance, the pup was resurrected, though still wobbley. He took two or three tentative steps, then beat a hasty retreat as Baron returned.

Now, Barney had several options. He could keep his cool. By glance and posture he could have told Baron, "Get lost, big bozo. I know you're all bluff." Or he could have made a show of courage, like preadolescents playing war games. I think Baron would have respected that. Or he could have extended the childlike leap-leap invitation to play. Barney did none of these. He just let his legs slide out from under him and, like a folding table, he collapsed.

Actually, he did more than just collapse. He totally flattened himself out, becoming a patch of fur too small and insignificant to be noticed. Besides, with his eyes tightly shut, how could he possibly be seen? For a long time Barney labored under the delusion that as long as he couldn't see what was coming, it wouldn't see him either.

Thus, posture became his standard defense against any and every threat. It's very difficult to punish a little puppy when he's all laid out flat like that. I guess you might say we spoiled him.

Baron, however, imposed upon the pup a stern and consistent discipline. *His* undoing was pride.

While it seemed that Barney capitulated to his immense and grouchy "big brother," instinct will out, and I suppose the gods give an extra dose of cunning to the underdog when the contest is too unequal. Barney quickly discovered a way of defying the king even while he appeared to give homage.

Among wolves and dogs, the instinctive gesture of subservience involves a sideways approach by the underdog, and the delivery of half a dozen rapid licks to the side of the king's mouth. If there was no time for the "collapse and die" routine, Barney employed the lick-lick tactic.

Now, the gesture of mouth-licking completely disarms the larger dog. It displaces feelings of aggression, summoning up pride and perhaps even a certain protective love. Up wriggles the little pup, seeking only to glorify the master. "Oh, strong and beautiful one," lick-lick, "I am your slave." Lick-lick. "What is this lowly bit of dust before grandeur such as thine?"

The big dog sighs, lifts his head, and basks in

glory. That momentary pause is enough for the little dog to get away with murder. He'll snatch the bone, grab the toy, rush out the gate, jump into the car, greet the visitors—in other words, he'll be *first* (which in every sibling rivalry is very important for scoring points), because the king has arthritis, and that momentary diversion is all it takes to defeat him.

Thus, Barney, by subverting the ancient hierarchical signal for his own gain, gave Baron a run for his money—except at bedtime. As Lloyd had foreseen, that first night was to set the pattern for all future bedtimes.

Baron settled himself down on his dirty old mat. We placed Barney in his nice new doggie bed on the other side of the garage, with the cartons positioned all around as a barricade. Faster than we could turn, the puppy was out of the bed, the cartons were scattered, and the entire plan had to be abandoned.

"Let Baron handle it," Lloyd grumbled. "That puppy isn't behaving."

(Lloyd tends to draw conclusions like that. I tell him it's useless to expect animals to behave like people. He doesn't see it that way. Some people fight about their kids. We fight about our animals.)

At bedtime Barney naturally sought warmth, furry feelings, a canine heartbeat. He did not like the nice new bed with its undog-smelling cushions.

Baron, on the other hand, had grown accustomed to his old mat between the cars. At bedtime he liked peace and privacy. He did not think it amusing when the puppy made a leap over him and landed on his chest.

It happened once, then again. The third time Barney pounced on top, Baron let out a lionesque growl. His viselike jaws snapped together, and Barney's piercing cry went on and on, a wail that pleaded, "Help! Oh, help, he's eating me alive, *alive!*"

Barney emerged unscathed, but reeled back. A moment later he began a commando crawl toward his king. "Ah, warm body," he seemed to say with his rolling eyes, "we cuddle up together, yes?"

Baron gave him a sneer, a growl.

Starting from the rear, Barney again attempted togetherness.

Baron snarled.

At last Barney sidled up, eyes shut, stopping short of the big dog's hindquarters. He sighed deeply, lay down, and stretched out a paw just far enough to touch the tip of his "brother's" tail. It would have to suffice.

Each night thereafter it was the same. Eternally hopeful and hungry for love, Barney made advances, his eyes asking the question, "Tonight?"

"Not on your life, you flea-ridden, slobbering fur piece!" retorted Baron with a twist of the lip, a guttural growl.

Occasionally in the night we'd hear a single bark, a responding yelp. Lloyd would turn over in bed and mutter, "They're fighting again."

But in the morning—did our eyes deceive us, or was the evidence clear? On Baron's side was a small, glossy wet spot, the kind that babies—and puppies—make while blissfully salivating in their sleep.

You know, of course, what happened to that nice bed. The cushion got eaten up. The frame still stands wedged between the old magazine rack and the broken lawnmower. The cardboard boxes had to be broken up and given to the trash man—with an extra couple of bucks for his trouble.

4

I'M NOT SURE when it actually dawned on us that Barney was different. I mean *really* different. If he'd been a child his teachers would have called him "unusual."

Some of the things he did were cute—the first dozen times around. Our puppy loved water, just like the kennel-lady had said—oh yes, he didums! He'd watch me standing there with the hose, watering the fruit trees, filling up those basins nice and deep, and then . . . splash! The entire puppy leaped into the mudhole and rooted there, grunting ecstatically. I've never known a shepherd dog to be so enamored of water.

The moment I'd fill the water bowl, Barney would try to swim in it. Or he'd knock it over with a swipe of his paw. Poor Baron went around thirsty and panting. It was impossible to keep the water bowl full. I turned my mind to inventing the perfect no-knock-over water pail, with visions of taking out a patent and becoming rich and famous—after all, it's not everyone who can turn a problem into an opportunity.

My first thought was to place a brick in the bottom of the bowl. But I immediately began to worry. Was there such a malady as brick poisoning? I was too embarrassed to ask the vet, too worried to take a chance. Next I put the water bowl inside a macramé plant holder and tied it to our porch railing. Barney loved it. He almost gave up baths for showers. Back to the drawing board. I invented a sturdy loop created from a wire coat hanger and fastened the bowl to a post. Barney dismantled that contraption in about two seconds.

I finally hit on the solution. It was so simple I wondered why I hadn't thought of it before: don't go anywhere, just stay around to fill the water bowl every hour or so.

Having been raised in a kennel, with only other puppies for company, Barney knew nothing of civilization. After all, what can one puppy teach another about living in a house or respecting a planted garden? The first time Barney noticed the patio window, he tried to ram his way through it. The hose he attacked as if it were a cobra. Inside the house, he seized the cushions from the sofa and proceeded to eat them.

We have an open-rail stairway leading down to our bedrooms. It never occurred to me that a puppy might dash headlong between the rails, for all animals, even insects, will cautiously test new terrain before stepping out. Not Barney. Someone left the front door open. Barney dashed into the house, and ran across the top stair and straight out into thin air. Down, down he went with a pitiful doomsday shriek, landing with such a horrible thud that as we rushed to the scene we feared all his bones were broken.

Ah, little animals—like little humans—are rubbery and resilient. Barney, receiving our kisses and recriminations, whimpered but a moment longer. Then he bounced up and cheerfully leaped into the toilet. We wondered for months afterward—had that terrible fall befuddled his brain?

Dan telephoned from college, asking for news, and was solemnly told by his father, "The new dog is a clown."

I defended Barney. "Children learn what they live," I said. "Dogs, too."

"Then let him learn not to be a clown," said Lloyd.

I was gratified to see that Barney did learn one thing immediately—how to walk on a leash. From the very first night, Barney was put on a leash and included in the nightly walk. He neither lunged ahead nor lagged behind. He moved like a windup toy, little legs swiftly propelling him forward, always within inches of Baron, who, of course, knew how to "heel."

We soon discovered the reason for Barney's apparent obedience; terror. He was scared of the dark, of the wind, of the trees, of water sprinklers, of pebbles, and of imagined animals that threatened to attack.

One night Barney's worst apprehensions came true. We rounded a corner. There stood another dog—a big dog. Barney froze stiff. In a twinkling he assessed the situation. *Zoom!* He sped forward, placed himself directly underneath Baron's body, running like crazy to match Baron's steady, complacent stride, gaining complete protection without losing mobility—oh, I was proud of his cleverness, even as I was convulsed with laughter. With the little dog so neatly tucked under the big dog, neither of them missing a step, it looked like an entirely new sort of beast, with eight legs.

Practically speaking, Barney's reticence (Lloyd called it cowardice) was no joke. Our would-be watchdog was turning into a regular Ferdinand the Bull. If anyone came to the gate, he took one desultory look, retreated to the mat in the corner, and let old Baron do the defending. He'd scratch himself or roll about or become very interested in a dry, fallen leaf, obviously having decided that he was the aesthetic type.

Occasionally, when the gardener came, Barney would join in with a bark or two, but you could tell it was an afterthought. He didn't really mean it. He had no intention whatsoever of putting his body on the line.

There were several other things he apparently had no intention of doing. Most of them were connected with toilet habits. I began to suspect he might have worms. The solution? Simple. Call the vet for an appointment. Put Barney in the car and take him to the vet.

We live on a hill. The vet is down in the village. Having Barney alone in the car with me that first time was—an adventure. I put him in the back seat, of course, started the motor, drove one block. Simple and smooth; the puppy was obviously enjoying the ride. I rounded a turn and began the descent gradually, of course, and was unperturbed.

But apparently Barney felt that the world was being pulled out from under him, for with a sudden leap he was upon me—not in the front seat on my lap, but clinging on to my back, *my back*, his forepaws tightly gripped around my head.

It is not easy driving down a steep hill with a large puppy hanging on to your head. I arrived at the vet's office a trifle shaken, struggling to keep my cool. (I've always considered it important to put up a good front for the vet, so that he won't think I'm one of those hysterical ladies who overindulge their pets, talk baby talk to them, and who can, therefore, be bilked out of thousands of dollars annually. So I act very nonchalant.)

Nonchalantly I sat there while Barney trembled, clamped his eyes shut, and in general made himself ridiculous, the laughingstock of the waiting room.

At last we were summoned—and found that our regular young vet had a new helper. Very young. Taciturn. This new vet was not at all jolly like the regular vet. Our regular vet, I learned, was jollying his way through Singapore, Thailand, and other wondrous points East. Last year at this time he was in Bali.

I was just beginning to draw some condemnatory conclusions when the new vet murmured, "Undernourished."

"He's so wild, Doctor!" I began to babble. "He doesn't mind, doesn't learn, won't go to the bathroom outside, messes up the patio, even eats his own . . ."

"Badly undernourished," said the vet. "Feel his bones. He's on the verge of rickets. And he's got a respiratory condition. In other words, a cold."

I was stunned. "But—but the kennel-lady," I stammered, "she told me—she keeps them thin on purpose. Rickets!"

The vet continued his examination. "You," he said, "bought him at a kennel?" Astonishment combined with contempt. It was my first inkling of the raging feud between vets and breeders.

"You might have asked us," he said with an injured air, then proceeded to write prescriptions with the urgency of a public-health inspector battling the plague.

"First he'll have to get a shot. Antibiotics and vitamins. Feed him daily multiple vitamins. And special food four times a day. Come back next week with a stool sample. Ten to one he's got worms."

"The kennel-lady," I ventured, "said she wormed him."

He gave me a withering look.

By the time we were finished, the vet had Barney wormed three times. It takes about three weeks for the worm's life cycle to progress from larva to egg-laying adult. If you don't catch all the larvae when they're in the stomach or the intestines the cycle starts anew. Three times for poor Barney. Maybe we were setting some kind of record.

After that first visit to the vet I carried my poor baby home. I was stunned and saddened. But I was not angry at the kennel-lady. She had apparently thought she was doing right, and I had not the proof or the knowledge to oppose her. One does not take a skinny puppy and return it like a defective lamp; one takes a puppy like a mate, for better or worse. And it did get worse, and even worse, to the point where I confided in the vet, young and taciturn though he might be.

I described Barney's behavior: "Doesn't learn. Chews up everything. Runs away when called. Scared of people. Scared of noises. A pest. A clown." Oh, I tried to be objective, but the complaints of those at home— even Dan, who'd come home for Christmas vacation— rang in my ears, and I had to admit that the consensus was well founded. Barney was a mess.

The vet nodded knowingly. "Well now, from what you tell me of the conditions where you got him, it would seem," he raised his brows, "that this dog, in his formative months, suffered some psychological trauma."

"What? *What?*" Surely he was putting me on. I seethed. College graduate that I am, student of psychology, rational and clearheaded human being, did he think I was going to fall for this kind of garbage?

"A puppy's social personality," he continued, "is molded somewhere between six and ten weeks of age. Like a baby, a puppy needs certain conditions if he is to develop normally with respect to his attitude toward other animals and toward humans."

32

Dazed, I cleared my throat and nodded slightly.

"This dog is obviously undersocialized," he said. "He obviously was not given enough human attention during a very critical time in his development. Therefore, he is fearful of humans and unable to cope with their requests."

"Definitely," I murmured, then added studiously, "Quite so."

He went on, tapping the puppy like some specimen. "For lack of a mother's prolonged presence, this puppy was too hungry for love, willing to subject himself to any authority, whether animal or human, and unable to stand up for his rights or to assume his responsibilities."

I whispered tearfully, "Doctor, what shall I do? Is there a cure?"

"Such damage could, perhaps, be overcome," he said soberly. "At times one can compensate and make the dog very nearly normal. But it takes a great deal of effort. It is," he concluded, "an enormous task."

Oh, the weight of it. I took him home. (Lloyd had informed me earlier that morning that Barney's vet bills were running up into the three-figure area.)

At home, I was eagerly plied with questions, including some by Lloyd's mother, who had come for her holiday visit.

"What's wrong with Barney?"

"Are the worms finally gone?"

"Did the vet say he'd stop eating his . . . ?"

"Why doesn't he behave?"

My mother-in-law, an inveterate shopper, kept asking, "Why don't you just exchange him? Why not? It doesn't seem fair to be stuck with a defective dog. Make that lady take him back. Did you at least get him on sale?"

I took my Barney out into the backyard and we escaped to our secret spot at the side of the house, where the ivy grows thick and you can be depressed without anyone bugging you.

Lloyd found us, finally, and gently he asked me what was the matter.

I whispered, "Barney was traumatized at a young age. He's got psychological problems."

Lloyd pulled me up, grinning. "Big deal. Who hasn't? Listen, maybe we can all go and get group therapy."

When he talks like that, I really know why I love him.

5

MORE AND MORE I noticed the disparity between old and young. Each morning when I took the two dogs to the vacant lot (the one to do his business, the other pretending he didn't know what on earth we were there for), I'd watch them. And it became clear that in every aspect of their behavior they were reflecting the universal, eternal truths about living, about youth and age, about beginnings and endings—about being a wise, dignified creature or a silly clown.

Run, leap, jump, snarl, dig, attack, play—that was

Barney's repertoire, all enacted in the span of time it took Baron to walk across the lot and gracefully lift his leg.

(It was still a cause of vexation to Lloyd and Dan that Barney urinated *like a girl dog!*)

Some people do everything harder, more fiercely, and in a more exaggerated manner than others. Some dogs are like that too. Let Barney scratch a flea and he'll thump against the floor like a power thresher. His kisses are extra slobbery, his drinking is the slurpiest I've ever heard, and if he lands a paw on a sensitive spot—forget it, you're out of commission till tomorrow.

Compared to every other puppy I've known, Barney was the feistiest, the most energetic. Mix that sort of personality with the sedentary temperament of a grumpy, retired army officer, and you see how it was between Barney and Baron.

"Come on! Play! What's wrong with you? Tumble, rumble, wrestle—*come on!*"

"Get lost."

"Please!"

"*I'll kill you!*"

I had to keep them separated for at least part of each day. Naturally, Barney got bored. Also, he had a certain talent that got him into trouble. If he had been human, he would definitely have become an archaeologist. He's a natural-born digger, finder, and collector of buried fossils.

Within the first two weeks of being let loose in our yard, Barney had uncovered every single bone that it had been Baron's pleasure, in the past three years, to bury or forget. An astonishing assortment of bones appeared, not strewn about haphazardly but laid out neatly on the deck that leads from our family room to the yard.

Now, as one might imagine, an array of dry bones piled in front of the door presents certain difficulties to persons going in and out. Especially at night, when it is dark.

Each morning I'd come out onto the deck and toss the dry bones back into the bushes. By noon they'd be collected again, with Barney beaming as if he'd just pulled 100% on the anthropology exam. I wised up. I began to collect the bones in a sack and throw them into the trash can. Somehow, they still multiplied. Barney began to fetch bones from earlier and earlier geologic ages.

When at last every old bone had been picked out of every bush and from beneath the soil, Barney met the challenge. He went to work on the rocks. It was a wise choice, for we live in Palos Verdes, famous for an abundance of rocks by that same name.

No matter what anybody says, every garden in Palos Verdes contains thousands of rocks, including large boulders. The local landscape architects label them "effective" and "artistic." The truth is, the boulders simply can't be moved without greater cost than anybody would care to contemplate. The small rocks are pushed behind waste bins or fences, but many still lie about and are likely to remain there until the next glaciation.

Barney, clever Barney, had a virtually endless supply of materiel. The sheer mass of matter might have discouraged a less dedicated collector. Not Barney. Hour after hour I'd see him slavishly fetching rocks and dumping them onto our wooden deck. Nor was it necessary to see him in order to be apprised of his progress. Rocks being dumped onto a wooden deck make a shocking noise—especially at night.

At night, while we watched TV, a low rumble would begin. Engrossed in a good plot, we'd ignore it. As the plot thickened, the rumble invariably increased, until the roar and rattle of the rocks was met by the ire of Lloyd. "What the *hell* is that dog doing out there? Why can't I ever watch TV in this house? First it's the rat, now that dog. I swear . . ."

The rat he referred to was, poor thing, long since dead, but it had been guilty of running on a squeaky exercise wheel each night precisely when the evening news came on. Now Barney was the culprit to be subdued, his beautiful collection of rocks and bones viciously confiscated. He would lie there, rolling his eyes mournfully, his body pressed tightly against the glass door, his expression saying, "You took away all my toys. I have nothing left to play with, and now you won't even let me come in and watch TV with you. Why do you hate me so much?"

The reason he couldn't watch TV was that he'd jump up into Lloyd's lap (and by now he surely weighed some seventy pounds), and Lloyd watches TV in one of those big reclining chairs, and when a big dog leaps onto the lap of a big man who is reclining as far back as the chair will go—well, you know what happens. And then *I* get yelled at.

Depressed, Barney became something of a necrophile, I'm afraid. He sniffed out and delivered to our doorstep the carcasses of numerous creatures I'll loosely term rodents. Exactly what they were was impossible to tell, due to their advanced state of decomposition.

I received his first offering with a shout and a shudder and hurled it far, far into the fields. The very next day, by some mastery of detective work, Barney rediscovered the carcass and once again presented it.

Birds fell victim to Barney's avocation. I found two dead in our front patio. Worse yet, one day I found only feet and tail feathers. It was a harrowing experience for one as squeamish as I. Naturally, Lloyd was at work, so the grisly task of disposal was left to me.

Of all the annoying proclivities common to dogs, I don't think Barney missed one. He dug out plants. He tore at the grass with his teeth. He shredded newspapers. He scratched out the screen door. He unwound every garden hose every single day. On top of that, he was the only dog I have ever known who could dig out an entire three-foot-tall rose bush, complete with wicked, piercing thorns, eat off every single bud and flower, grind the thing down to its root ball, and toss the remaining atrocity—you guessed it—onto the wooden deck. Nobody, not even Baron, wanted to go out into the backyard anymore.

Maybe Barney knew I was at the end of my rope. Maybe he knew that even I, who for some strange reason loved him, would no longer put up with his misdeeds unless he were to exhibit some saving grace. At any rate, in April, when he'd been with us seven months, Barney committed the deed that, temporarily at least, vindicated him and saved his hide. He single-handedly saved the lives of two fellow creatures—kittens.

6

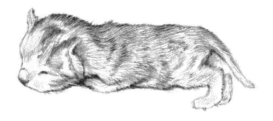

I HAD BEEN out shopping. Joan, the high-school girl who cleaned house for me some afternoons, met me at the door, wringing her hands.

"Barney dug something up," she said, pointing out the window to the deck below. "I think it's a rat." She shuddered. "I think it's dead."

She then became intent on her dust cloth, obviously wishing to remove herself from any possible suggestion that she dispose of the thing. I stepped closer to the window, gazed down, let out a gasp, and simultaneously grabbed a shoe box from the table.

"Joan! I don't think it's a rat!" I began to run down the stairs, with Joan following. "It's . . . I think it's . . ."

Outside, I bent over it, a moist, motionless little clump of gray fur, and just as I began pondering what kind of creature this was, dying or dead, it let out a long, sharp "Meow!"

That meow—I hear its echo still as it touched and pierced my being, saying to me with the utmost clarity and conviction, "Oh, help me! I only want to live and become a cat!"

I picked up the tiny body and hastily laid it in the shoe box, on top of the dust cloth I'd taken from Joan's hand. We got Barney out of the yard and up into the front patio, then proceeded to search for possible additional survivors of what was obviously a new litter.

Sure enough, we found another kitten lying on the step below the deck, this one definitely weaker than the first, its head hanging limply to one side so that it seemed its back and neck were broken.

Alternatives flashed through my mind, along with all sorts of implausible explanations as to how the kittens happened to be here in my yard with Barney—until all other thoughts were overwhelmed by the certainty that I must get these kittens to the vet. I simply couldn't cope alone. Maybe their necks were indeed broken. Maybe Barney had crunched them to death. *Go to the vet!*

"We're going to the vet," I told Joan, who opted for kitty-sitting instead of cleaning, and we drove down the hill, the kittens in the shoe box between us.

When we got there, we ran inside and confronted the bewildered receptionist.

"I think these are kittens," I gasped.

"They are," she said, peering into the box.

"I need to see the vet."

"He's gone."

"Gone? You mean—far? To Hong Kong?"

"Out to lunch. He'll be back at three."

"I can't wait!" I shouted. "What'll I do?" I explained my dilemma.

She gently suggested that I call the ASPCA, and added, "If they were just left in your yard, it's not really your responsibility."

I stared at her. "The ASPCA?" I echoed stupidly. "They won't take care of the kittens. They'll kill them!"

"Well, yes," she agreed, "but what else can you do?"

"Would you look at them?" I asked. "Tell me if they're all right? I've never had kittens. . . ."

"I wouldn't even want to touch them," she said,

shaking her head. "They're too tiny." She used the patient tone of a kindergarten teacher. "If you like, I'll phone the animal shelter for you."

I noticed her change of terminology. The result would be the same. Unless I . . . "I'll take them home," I said, "and feed them."

Wordlessly, she reached under the counter and brought out an eyedropper and a little book titled *The Care of Orphaned and Abandoned Kittens.* The book was proof to me, at least, that saving kittens was not so unique or insane an idea as the receptionist's stare indicated.

"I guess I could use two eyedroppers, please."

She obliged, and we departed.

Home again, I finally found the courage to examine the orphans, and discovered that one still had a twiglike thing attached to its abdomen. I realized that if the umbilical cord was still attached, their mamma really *had* split in a hurry.

For several days afterward, questions continued to be asked and answers were vainly sought. I now called the next vet on my list, a woman with a mobile unit. It was her day off. I sighed as I realized that fate had tapped me, personally, on the shoulder, and I proceeded to heat up some milk, adding a few grains of sugar.

44

I took the kittens by turns, each wrapped in a bit of cloth, to lie on their back in the palm of my hand. They were as unattractive as little mice, their fur matted, eyes sealed. At last I succeeded in pressing the eyedropper into their tiny pink mouths. They neither sucked nor grasped the dropper, but, miraculously, they did swallow. After two dropperfuls each, I tucked the babies back into the shoe box and tried to think. It was about four in the afternoon. So far, my ordeal had lasted about three hours. I felt exhausted.

Lloyd and I were going to a potluck buffet dinner that night. I had promised to come early and help set up. I'd have to hurry and dress, set up the tables, rush back home to meet Lloyd, and meanwhile the kittens . . .

Outside, the weather had changed from merely chilly to a gusty, biting cold. The eucalyptus trees across the street were bent low under the force of the wind, and from the smell in the air, I knew we'd have a hard, driving rain by nightfall.

I ran out into the backyard, calling, "Kitty! Here, Kitty!" Of course, I found no postpartum cat waiting to reclaim her litter. I went out onto the street, calling, crooning, seeking the one I knew even then would not appear, and as I walked in the biting wind I cursed her, enraged at all mothers who are selfish and negligent, who leave their offspring to become the charges of others, who want to dance to the tune but refuse to pay the piper. Oh, I worked up a very fine rage against this debauched vagrant of a mother cat. Inwardly I raged, while I forced my countenance into a placid mask, calling into every shrub and corner, "Kitty! Kitty-kitty-kitty!"

At this point I must explain that I had never before talked to cats. In my whole life I had had no traffic whatsoever with cats, except to peer at the lions in the zoo. So, for me to be prowling the windy streets in search of a mother cat was not only aggravating but ludicrous.

"Kitty-kitty-kitty!" At last! I spotted a cat. It immediately bounded away through the thicket in the canyon. Another cat came ambling by, unsuspecting. I managed to grab it, and was about to deliver a scathing lecture on sense of responsibility, when I noticed, to my dismay, that in no way could it be a mother. It stalked off, tail switching angrily. Later, I learned that he was a seventeen-year-old neutered male.

Home once again, I took up the telephone, determined to call every neighbor whose number I had garnered over the years. As I telephoned, I was mindful of the time—it was four-thirty. I spoke softly to my neighbors while in my heart brandishing a big stick, for one of them, no doubt, had perpetrated this foul deed.

The first one I called, Mrs. Clausenstock, confirmed my suspicion. "My dear," she said, "somebody probably dropped them in your yard. We? Oh, we have no cats. Haven't had cats in years. Dear me, no."

The Firnwoods down the street had cats, but they were "males, only males." As for the Johnsons, their cat wasn't really *their* cat: oh, no, it really belonged to the Kirkhams, around the corner, and they hadn't seen that cat in a year or so. At least a year. And she *was* sorry.

I discovered, to my amazement, that not one person in our entire neighborhood had ever owned a female cat, nor wished to own one, nor had seen one in the last thirty days. Apparently all the cats had stopped propagating. Or some freak plague had wiped out all the females. Sure.

I wised up and started phoning not the mothers but the kids. One seven-year-old boy confessed that yes, the Mulligans *did* have a mother cat, and yes she *was* expecting. Eureka!

Mrs. Mulligan, a good, churchgoing woman, laughed heartily when I suggested that perhaps her cat had dropped a litter in my yard and would she please come over to identify and claim the kittens. "Kittens? Cats? Pregnant? Ha-ha-ha." I was mistaken. Her cat wasn't even there. As a matter of fact, her cat was dead—yes, dead.

Mrs. Mulligan further advised me, in no uncertain terms, that cats never abandon their babies. They *never* drop their litters in fenced yards where a German shepherd is standing guard. Furthermore, if they do misplace a kitten or two, they will always return for it very, very soon.

I thanked Mrs. Mulligan, noted that it was now five o'clock, and wrote a note for Shari, who was off on some afterschool adventure of her own and still did not know the specifics of my afternoon. "Two kittens are on counter in box," I scribbled. "Feed with eyedropper. I'll explain when I get home at seven."

Hastily I brushed my hair, pulled on a decent pair of slacks and a sweater, and thumbed through the cat-care book while I stepped into my shoes and collected my things.

The book said to keep the kittens warm.

How? Desperately I racked my brain. However, the writers of that marvelous little book had foreseen the emotional state of one who finds herself suddenly with abandoned kittens. They had spelled out everything: "Keep the kittens warm. Use a heating pad or a hot-water bottle."

48

Joy! I knew exactly where the heating pad was. I found it, placed it under the shoe box, turned it on low, and sped out the door.

Oh, God. I'd forgotten my contribution to the pot-luck. I had planned to make one of those gorgeous salads, with stuffed eggs, anchovies, curled carrots, thinly sliced cucumbers, and other delectable goodies. I ran back and flung open the cupboard door, to find half a dozen boxes of dry cereal and, on the top shelf, an unopened bottle of bourbon.

I made the obvious choice.

7

A F T E R H E L P I N G T O set up the buffet, I dashed home, and no sooner had I thrust my key into the lock than the telephone rang. It was Mother. I told her, hastily, about the kittens.

Mother's usual tone of voice is weak and martyred, so that her wayward children will worry whether she'll make it through the night. Her voice now took on a rare quality of delight, then staunch determination.

"We must save them," she said.

"We?" I echoed. "Would you be interested in helping?"

"Yes, yes!" she cried. "Poor, motherless babes. They must be fed, nursed, kept warm."

"You will do that?" I inquired.

"Of course. Just bring them to my apartment to-morrow."

"Oh, I will! And bless you, Mother."

Five minutes later the telephone rang again. It was Mother. Her neighbor Esther had informed her that one could not possibly feed newborn kittens adequately with an eyedropper. Furthermore, Esther had had ample experience with such matters and knew for a fact that the kittens' mother would come looking for them. Therefore, Esther had concluded, the kittens must be put out into the backyard immediately and left there for the mamma cat to claim.

Besides, Mother added, it was too much work to take care of newborn kittens. Anyhow, her landlord would probably throw her out. On top of that, she hadn't been feeling well. However, she assured me that if she were twenty years younger she would be happy to do it.

I thanked Mother for her information and good intentions, then went to find Shari, who was sitting on the floor in her room, talking on her telephone to someone who was seemingly hard-of-hearing.

"Did you see my note?"

"I'm on the phone," she chided me, nice and loud.

"I'm leaving again in ten minutes!" I screamed. "Get off that phone. Talk to me! Did you feed the kittens?"

"Of course I did," she said, bored; and to her friend, "Lisa, I gotta go. My mom's after me. Again."

Yes, she had seen the note. For the first half hour she had ignored it.

"Why, pray tell?"

"You often write crazy notes," she said. "I thought it was a joke. I just went ahead and fixed myself a snack. Later, I happened to look inside the box and I saw the kittens and I fed them."

That was all. No gasps of joy. No admiration. No begging, "Oh, Mother, can we keep them? Can we?"

I related the entire episode—how I'd found the kittens, dashed to the vet's, sought the mother cat, fed them . . . I guess secretly I hoped she'd nominate me Mother of the Year.

Shari said, "It was good that you brought them inside. Listen, I've got to go now. I've got to call Karen." Without further conversation she took the shoe box and the heating pad from the kitchen and installed the kittens in her room.

Minutes later Lloyd rushed in frazzled and dazed

from his freeway commute and slightly irritable from hunger and the prospect of having to get ready to go out. If it were up to men, potluck dinners would be banished from the world, along with scout meetings and the annual Father-Daughter Tea.

While Lloyd was dressing, I told him briefly and unemotionally about the kittens.

He said nothing.

I told him how I'd searched for the mother cat.

He said nothing.

I told him about my mother's phone call and Esther's suggestion.

He said, "Esther is right. The mother cat will return. We must definitely put the kittens outside and give the mother a chance to find them."

I said, "You're right. That's very logical. Maybe they're too young and frail to live without a mother."

Lloyd was pleased at the maturity of my attitude. He added, "By putting them out for the mother to find, we at least give them a chance to survive."

I asked, "What if the mother cat doesn't come for them?"

He frowned. "She probably will," he said, though he sounded dubious, and repeated, "She probably will."

We walked downstairs together. On the way we met Shari and explained that the kittens must be put outside so that their mother could find them. It was the correct thing to do. We must not interfere with Nature and Instinct. We were, after all, not responsible. We had brought those kittens in out of the cold, given them a free meal, searched for their mother . . . it was enough. Now we must be sensible.

Outside, it was raining now, harsh, oblique sheets of water that came slanting under the roof overhang even onto our deck. The wind was bending even the sturdiest branches, smacking leaves against our windows. A door creaked somewhere. I thought I heard the roll of thunder in the distance.

I said, "The kittens will get wet out there."

"We'll set them on the deck, under the roof," said Lloyd. "They won't get too wet."

Shari said, "According to the little book Mommy got, the kittens are supposed to be kept warm. Eighty-five degrees. Right now they're lying on the heating pad."

"So we'll wrap them up before we put them out," Lloyd declared, glancing at his watch. "Hurry, now! If they're strong, they'll survive. If not . . . well, that's Nature. Darwin. Where are those kittens?"

On Shari's lips I saw a slight smile, feminine and tender. She gently held out her hand and said, "Come on, Dad, they're in my room."

54

Shari led the way. On her desk was the shoe box, lined with the heating pad. The cord, plugged into the wall, stretched like a lifeline straight to the two tiny gray bodies, now fluffy and nearly dry, sleeping pressed together head to tail, their breathing declaring, "Alive! Alive!" but their utter exhaustion indicating, "just barely."

They had been through a terrible ordeal—dropped by a careless mother in a damp garden, carried in the mouth of a huge German shepherd, tossed out onto the deck and the rocks below, mauled a bit, perhaps. . . .

"They've only just dried out," Shari whispered.

A spatter of rain rolled across the bedroom window.

Lloyd stood motionless, looking down into the box. He stared. Then he shut his eyes tight, the way Barney does when things get too overwhelming, and he called out, "No! No! I can't do it!" He began to pace. "We'll feed them. We'll nurse them. Even if I have to take them to work with me. How can I put them out in the rain?"

I wept. Shari wept. We three stood in her bedroom, clinging to one another, and then I whispered to Lloyd, "I love you. They only want to be *cats*."

So it was settled. We'd keep the kittens just long enough to wean them from the eyedropper to the nursing bottle and then to solid food. Then we'd find good homes for them. Because we already had a pony, a hamster, a fish, and Baron and Barney. We didn't even care for cats. We had always been dog people, never wanted cats. We'd do those kittens a good turn, get them started, and then, at the appointed time, bid them good luck and farewell.

Lloyd and I went off to the potluck dinner secure and happy with our plan. We had committed ourselves to nothing more than giving some milk to a couple of kittens for a few weeks.

As if he needed reassurance that we'd soon send them packing, Lloyd reminded me, "You've always been allergic to cats. Remember? Remember how you'd start sneezing and your eyes would itch whenever we visited the Fosters?"

I remembered.

8

IT SEEMED LIKE a simple undertaking. Shari promised to do night feeding. That first night I prepared warm milk in a thermos and placed it, with the kittens, the eyedroppers, and clean newspapers and cloths, beside Shari's bed. She set her alarm clock for 2:00 A.M. I felt like a new mother who has just hired a practical nurse to take care of her infant—very ambivalent, mostly worried.

But I forced myself to be calm as I got ready for bed. If Lloyd suspected my nervousness, he'd say it was all too much for me. He'd recount episodes where I'd gotten "overextended," which is one of his words. So I played it cool.

I caught him at 6:00 A.M., dressed in his robe and slippers, trying to sneak back into the bedroom. I sat bolt upright, dreading to ask, for they were so very frail. He smiled that embarrassed smile. "They're alive," he said. "They're crying for their breakfast. Shari's feeding them."

I lay back with a sigh and an overwhelming feeling of relief. This, I thought, was a miracle. Once we had tried to save a tiny, orphaned mouse; it had died in my hand after a long night.

But these kittens—what fine babies! They had even slept through the night. This was going to be easier than I'd thought. According to the book, kittens could be weaned in four weeks. By then I'd have found good homes for them. Meanwhile, I would follow that little yellow book as years ago I had followed Dr. Spock.

At first I had hesitated at the very idea of raising any animal without a mother. Would they be burdened for life with hang-ups and complexes like my poor Barney? By some strange coincidence, just two months before, Dan had sent me a psychology study titled "Social Deprivation in Monkeys."*

---

* Harry F. and Margaret Kuenne Harlow, *Scientific American*, Nov. 1962.

He had sent it, knowing my interest in both psychology and animal behavior, and, I suppose, to prove he was actually doing something there at MIT besides building a twenty-foot electronic yo-yo. At any rate, the article explained that infant monkeys who are deprived of a mother can still grow up normal in every way as long as they socialize with other monkeys their own age. The company of a peer group, not a mother, was essential to the monkeys' development.

I concluded that the same must apply to kittens. All I had to do was to provide the usual necessities.

I soon discovered that kittens are not so very different from human babies. They cry to be fed about every four hours, shaking their little heads in rage. They would soil their diapers if they had any. When they're full, their tummies get round and their faces take on that sleepy, puckered look. They nuzzle toward anything soft and warm—a toy doggie, each other, or a person wearing a sweater.

Like any mother of twins, I soon learned to feed by rotation. Later on, visitors were encouraged—nay, *required*—to help. Four or five times daily I'd sit with the kittens, taking each in turn into the palm of my hand, wrapped in a buntinglike tissue, while I carefully squeezed milk drop by drop into the little pink mouth.

As I sat there at the kitchen table feeding them,

then burping them (oh yes, that too), I became strangely oblivious to such crises and grievances as soaring gasoline prices, presidential blunders, teenage frenetics, and the snails feasting nightly on my petunias. My total absorption in the task at hand felt a bit familiar.

Familiar too was that sense of heightened urgency as I began each new day. There was so much to do! Priorities changed. How could I possibly go out to lunch? I had babies to feed. I had to worry about whether they ate too much or too little, got bloated or dehydrated, were too hot or too cold. Who else could interpret their cries of hunger, pain, or boredom? I had to examine their stool (the little book said so!), inspect their fur, shield them from drafts, keep obstreperous children away, and deal tactfully with the dogs, who displayed typical sibling jealousy along with the desire to help. Barney was the most eager. Unfortunately, his ideas of parenting were completely at odds with mine. So, I had to keep the kittens in their shoe box high up on the kitchen counter, and soothed Barney's and Baron's feeling with extra pats, kisses, and goodies.

Each night I patiently explained to Lloyd that yes, of course, I was still on the lookout for that vagrant mother cat. Was it my fault she was obviously some out-of-towner, here only long enough to drop her litter?

Lloyd almost accused me of enjoying this catastrophe.

Enjoying? Ha—I had plenty of other things to do, thank you. I was merely fulfilling a responsibility that some higher power had seen fit to foist upon me.

"I've heard you," he said, "talking to those cats."

"Pure falsehood," I retorted.

Why, I'm the one who has always taken a low view of women who baby-talk to animals, who croon, "Mamma loves you, yes she does!" "Neurotics," I'd called them, and "frustrated old maids."

I guess I had become complacent, relaxed. Maybe I was talking to myself. Once Shari came upon me and asked in astonishment, "Mother, are you aware that you are *purring?*"

"Nonsense," I told her. "Go clean your room."

Shari and Lloyd whispered about me. They said I was changing. Actually, they were the ones. Shari was finally getting more self-reliant, leaving me to my duties. And Lloyd, poor man, went shuffling around the house with that displaced, baffled expression on his face, that look I've seen before when men find themselves caught in a woman's domain, be it the beauty salon, boutique, or nursery.

He expressed his frustration in the form of questions. "What's all this costing me, anyhow?"

Many years of marriage have taught me the value of evasion. I executed a very equivocal shrug. Actually, I was feeding those kittens Queen's Milk Substitute, as recommended by the book. This creamy concoction comes in a can and costs roughly as much as Russian caviar or French champagne. I chose not to discuss such trivia.

"What's happened to your allergy?" he persisted.

I know how to assume a vague, moronic expression that implies a total lack of comprehension. In truth, I couldn't figure out why I wasn't itching, sneezing, and coughing. Maybe the kittens were still too young to be harmful.

For his *coup de grace* Lloyd demanded, "What about our vacation?"

I returned question for question. "Don't you think they'll be gone by then? Don't you think I've got that all worked out?"

I soothed him. "This is so good for Shari. It will teach her patience and responsibility." That one did the trick.

It did take patience. It meant rising early to feed the kittens before making the family breakfast. After the beds were made and the dishes done, it was time for the kittens' bath.

Yes, bath. During the night kittens get messy and

malodorous. They need to be bathed with pure soap and warm water, then rinsed, and dried thoroughly lest they catch pneumonia. Then, to stimulate their circulation, the kittens had to be brushed. I used a beat-up old toothbrush.

After every feeding came another necessity—elimination. The little book had informed me that kittens don't do it naturally. The mother cat gently licks them, which stimulates this function. When the kittens have no mother, the surrogate must lend a hand. So, after each feeding, we'd apply a damp tissue to the kittens' bottoms, gently stroking until we got results.

I didn't realize quite how involved I had become until the day my friend Linda dropped in. We were making the transition from eyedropper to bottle. I'd been standing in the kitchen for over an hour, trying to punch the right-size holes into those recalcitrant rubber nipples.

I explained my plight to Linda. She stared at me, baffled, then burst out laughing.

"What's wrong?" I asked. "What's funny?"

She laughed even more. "Well," she said, "you certainly don't have an empty nest anymore."

"Now really," I objected, and I was going to tell her, "Listen, I'm no dummy, I know all about displace-

ment and other psychological mechanisms of need ful-
fillment," but instead I gazed at her and nodded
sheepishly. How could I deny it? She knew the empti-
ness I'd felt after Dan left for college. Oh, I'd put on a
bold front and a big grin, and I didn't allow myself
to brood over that empty room, but I had to admit that
a great need in me had suddenly been filled in the most
unexpected, remarkable way.

"No more empty nest," I agreed. And all the rest
of the day I reflected upon this insight: there are some
cravings that the intellect alone cannot satisfy.

Before she left, Linda asked, "Are you going to
keep them?"

"Of course not!" I replied somewhat indignantly.

Again she laughed.

9

I LIKE TO think of myself as the sort of person who takes things pretty much in stride. Friends sometimes praise my calm, easygoing disposition. It's all a front. Actually, I'm beset by ambivalence. I talk a lot about change and growth, but endings disturb me.

Take the weaning of the kittens—a perfectly natural and desired event, right? Oh boy! I'd be done with those monotonous bottle-feedings and bottom-wipings, that total dependency. True. But it was also true that I wasn't in a hurry to give up my babies. With mixed emotions, I bought them a litter box and thought ahead to solid food.

I did look forward to the big day when the kittens would open their eyes. For the first couple of weeks they were just furry little blobs, undifferentiated, their faces obscure. How would they look with their eyes open? And how would we look to them? The first time for anything is such an adventure! Shari and I couldn't wait for them to see the world for the first time, and when the day came it was even better than we'd imagined.

The smaller of the kittens, the one with the tiny gray face, was the first to reveal the faintest slit of a pale gray-green eye. Only for an instant could we see it, then the eyes were sealed again, and all day that kitten seemed to be practicing, gradually allowing itself to see, blinking, peering, staring.

The other kitten—the plump, gray-and-white-striped one—was entirely different. There must be two sorts of hatchlings in every species, those who peck careful little cracks in their eggs, who emerge a whisper at a time from shell or mud or mamma, and those who break out shouting with gusto. So it was with our two kittens. The first was timid and reluctant; the second opened its eyes all at once, and they were huge and sparkled like lanterns.

66

I had just finished bottle-feeding this one. One moment its eyes were blissfully shut, the next they were wide open, and the kitten gave a start. Its eyes suddenly engaged my face as it sat upright and gave me a long, penetrating stare, thrust its head forward to get a clearer focus on my face, then cocked its head in that universal expression of amazement, as if to say, "Good heavens, are *you* my mother? What about your whiskers? Your fur? Your very *catness?*"

In the next instant it stepped toward me, then nuzzled very close, and a full, throaty purr took over its entire body. It was a purr of total contentment. Yes, I was all right with this kitten. Instinct had naturally led it to expect paws and claws and tail. But it surely recognized my smell, voice, and touch. Here it had found warmth and sustenance and love. How else does one define "Mother"?

That night, when Lloyd came home from work and saw the open-eyed kittens, he peered anxiously into the little one's face. "It's all glassy-eyed," he stated.

I had noticed it too—a bleary look. "Maybe that's because they've just opened," I said hopefully.

The next morning, after he'd left, I found this note on the kitchen table: "Maybe kitty needs glasses. Take it to the eye doctor. Keep bedroom door closed. They'll start walking through the house now."

He was right. Now, when we set them down, the kittens began to explore, and it was a delight to watch their discoveries. They played with each other's tails and paws and ears. They captured and pounced on odd little things like half a peanut shell or a paper clip or a cracker. They moved together, finding security in each other, obeying some instinct that told them they needed each other in this large house—each needed the other as a mirror and as a teacher. In a moment they would move from pouncing play to sound sleep, usually on the stairs where they could press their little bodies securely against the carpet and catch a bit of sun from the window. They were so sweet; my mother would come especially to see them.

At the potluck dinner I had told everyone about the kittens, asking them to please remember me should anybody be looking for a good mouser. After about three weeks, my friend Gail telephoned with news of a possible home for one of the kittens. Her neighbor's cat had been killed by a car and she wanted a new kitten. So, Gail wanted to come and see ours.

I told Shari that Gail was coming. I laid it all out for her. It was nearly time to give them away. We had to be sensible.

"Which one does she want?" Shari asked. "Jesse?"

I felt a flash of panic. "What do you mean, *Jesse!* Who's Jesse?"

"Well, I've been calling the bigger one Jesse," she said. "Don't you like that name?"

"It's irrelevant whether I like the name or not," I snapped. "Who said you should name them, anyhow? I wasn't planning to name them."

"Well, I just did it—for myself, you know," Shari said, more sweetly than is her habit. "I keep trying to think of a name for the other one. Maybe Jesse and Tessie? She's so tiny, all gray. I'm sure she's a girl, aren't you?"

We had made several diagnostic attempts in this area, and concluded that the larger of the kittens—the one with the white markings—was male, and the smaller was a female.

I pondered. "If I were naming her, I'd pick Tinkerbell or Pixie or . . ." Then I had it. "Jinx," I said. "I would call her Jinxie. Jinxie and Jesse."

When Gail came, Shari introduced her to the kittens. "This is little Jinxie," she said tenderly, placing the tiny gray kitten on my friend's lap. "Jinxie is delicate. She's nervous. She needs extra care."

Gail nodded in obvious agreement. "Maybe you'd rather keep the stronger one, then," she said. "What's its name?"

"Jesse," I said.

Two days later Gail called back. "My neighbor is willing to take the little gray one," she told me, "the smaller one, you know. I had the feeling you'd rather keep the larger one. It might turn out to be healthier and—"

"What?" I cried, in spite of myself. "She wants to take Jinxie? No, no, she's too small, too delicate and nervous. Jinxie needs . . ."

"Well then," Gail said amicably, "I suppose my neighbor won't mind taking the larger one. Actually she might prefer it."

"But how can I give you Jesse?" I exclaimed. "Jinx depends on Jesse. They're inseparable."

I looked around distractedly, only to catch sight of Shari leaning in the doorway, with a sly smile only half concealed.

Drat that child! I knew we shouldn't have named them.

"Then, do you mean you've changed your mind?" Gail asked. "You're keeping the kittens?"

"I guess I haven't really decided," I mumbled. "We're going on vacation soon," I added lamely, and, "Shari's gotten so attached to them."

I hung up feeling rotten and elated all at once. More elated than rotten, really. In fact, more as if skyrockets were going off around me. For now, at least, I could play Scarlett O'Hara and face it "tomorrow." Our vacation wasn't due until June. Lloyd assumed the kittens would be gone, while I was weighing the relative merits of kennel versus kitty-sitter. It just goes to show you how two people living in the same house can be on completely different wavelengths.

On the one hand I suppose I tried to ignore their steady growth; on the other hand it was such fun to watch each new stage of their development. How readily they accepted the litter box, as if they had been born knowing about it. How politely they sampled the milk and the baby-food chicken I set out for them, and how immediately after their first proper meal, they began washing.

They had, of course, long since outgrown the shoe box, and had progressed to a succession of larger cartons until they were kept in the area behind the bar in our family room.

That bar—in our younger days, we fancied ourselves owning a built-in bar as a symbol of that chic, success-leisure image we admired. By the time we got our bar, we'd given up drinking as well as images, the one because it's fattening, the other because they're a bore. Thus, the bar has been variously used as a workbench, an artist's table, and a home for whatever pets could no longer be tolerated elsewhere. In, on, under, and behind the bar have lived hamsters, some fish, that poor little mouse, a rabbit (that was only a one-night stand), and then the kittens.

Within a couple of days after they got their vision,

Jinx and Jesse developed wanderlust. Jesse led the way. First it was out of the box, then up and over the barricade, which daily grew more challenging and more preposterous.

At night particularly, Lloyd wants to have each animal nicely in its place. The fish in its bowl never objects. The hamster has no choice. And the dogs are content to sleep when we do. But kittens happen to be nocturnal. Their very best games begin at night—leaping, tumbling, free-for-all frolicking—which made Lloyd holler, "Look at those kittens! Why don't they *behave?*"

"They are behaving," I'd say coolly. "They're behaving like cats. That," I'd explain, "is a game called 'jungle cat.' "

"They are not allowed to play that game," Lloyd would persist. "Not this late at night. Tell them to go to sleep."

"Kitties! Go to sleep."

They refused. They kept leaping out over the bar. At last we decided to lock them in the den at night, along with their litter box, food, water, newspaper, and a blanket. Each night, then, came the kitten hunt—getting Jesse down off the drapery rods, finding Jinxie behind the refrigerator, or inside the clothes dryer, or behind the fake wall she had discovered behind the paneling in the family room. It was an ordeal, I tell you.

Why couldn't they sleep in the bathroom? Too small.

Why not in the kitchen? Unsanitary. And they might just turn on the burners—don't ask me how.

How about the hallway? Too near our bedroom. Shari's room? No, they'd bother her.

Dan's room? It was empty anyhow. Oh no, it wouldn't be fair to Dan to invade his privacy, and his being three thousand miles away didn't make any difference. It was a matter of principle.

But why not just let them roam at will? Other people do. Listen, the Joneses, the Mulligans, the Mortons, the Leonis—they all have cats and they all let them roam the house at night. NOBODY PUTS CATS TO BED IN A ROOM. NOBODY, DO YOU HEAR?

We had a terrible fight. Not a tiff or a spat or an argument or a discussion or anything halfhearted like that, but a drag-out fight that lasted for hours.

Lloyd did not like it. This was his home. His home was supposed to be his castle. His castle had become a zoo. He had to fight his way into the patio each night, with one dog leaping for his jugular, the other slapping at his expensive business suit with tongue and tail, then sinking down with a groan at his feet, and

73

the two kittens rushing nimbly to beat him into the bedroom the moment the door was opened the slightest crack. There was dog dirt on the lawn, cat hair on the counters, and now—now he couldn't even *sleep.*

We compromised. The kittens would sleep in the den.

I didn't mind the mess—oh no. The den just happens to be the place where I write. And I am, besides a zoo keeper, a writer.

It's strange to note, in retrospect, how policy is made and habits are born. For months—in fact, until long after we had returned from our vacation—I continued to bed those cats down in my den each night, and each morning I would undo the damage. Eventually in a burst of inspiration, I had a talk with a vet.

I vividly recall her diagnosis. "Those kittens," she said, "have got you guys wrapped around their little fingers."

"Paws," I argued weakly.

"Paws," the vet acknowledged, then added, "Who's running your house?"

I didn't answer. I knew who.

10

I'M NOT SURE when it finally dawned on Lloyd that the kittens weren't leaving. We never actually discussed it. When it came time to go on our vacation, I pointed out that it seemed silly to make them leave the house when we were leaving anyhow. We had to make arrangements for Baron and Barney during our absence, so why not include the kittens?

We usually had one of the kids in the neighborhood run over twice a day to feed the dogs. Now I mused, wasn't it shocking how many robberies occurred while people were out of town? An empty house was easy prey to vandals and thieves. And wasn't it awful that an entire garden could go brown for lack of attention during even so short a spell as just two weeks? Oh yes, empty houses are bad news. House plants die. Ants and roaches move in. And in case of fire from faulty wiring, why, the whole house can burn down in no time.

What to do? Well, how would I know? But it just so happened, as an interesting bit of information, that Dagmar, that nice high-school girl down the street, was having problems with her family as a result of her ambition to play the clarinet. Poor Dagmar needed a place to practice.

Lloyd had a perfectly wonderful idea. Couldn't Dagmar house-sit for us?

The next day I called Dagmar to confirm our plans. Then I began to make lists. This is a holdover from when the kids were little. It's also a way of coping with separation anxiety. I get that way whenever I have to pack a suitcase. Formerly my lists included emergency numbers, car-pool schedules, and vital tips such as Dan's refusal to bathe without bubbles and Shari's aversion to foods that wriggle, as well as foibles of my household appliances.

Lists like this are embarrassing. You can go along

for years picking up all sorts of odd little habits and never think anything of it. Then comes a sitter, and all those idiosyncrasies stand glaringly exposed. I must make a trade-off: peace of mind for letting the sitter see how I have allowed myself to fall victim to a thousand small tyrannies imposed by myself or by others. It's all there in the list:

> Garage door doesn't shut tight. Tie it down
> with a rope.
> Dust Jinxie with flea powder, but don't let
> Jesse lick it off.
> Whack the refrigerator if it goes off.
> Give Baron pink medicine (for diarrhea),
> boiled rice, and broth, and milk in the
> morning when he says "Awhoof-awhoo."
> Barney gets burrs in his snout. Use tweezers.

The tweezers were taped to the wall, along with the neatly typed list. In the ensuing predeparture panic, I always remember dozens of extra items, which I then proceed to scribble out and affix to the original list, until the final document is a collage of objects and harried notations.

Milk comes twice a week. Feed house plants Monday. Barney won't go toilet on leash. Use long rope kept in green box under kitchen counter. Baron won't

77

walk on leash at all. Let him follow along. Take in mail.
Give bones to dogs. No chicken bones. Give eggs to all
animals sometime. On Sunday water potted plants.
Give Barney some tennis balls.

Before leaving home, I am seized with another sort
of craziness. Suddenly I get clean. I take up torn hems,
sew on buttons, plow through the kitchen junk drawer,
donate old clothes to Goodwill, and throw out all the
bottles I've been saving to do something creative with.
(I have never yet found the time or the creative use for
some two-dozen assorted bottles. I keep thinking I will.)

What makes me do it? Naked fear. What if I die
while I'm away? Bereaved friends, family, and neighbors will tiptoe into my empty house, and in their grief
they will whisper, "Oh, she was such a sweet person—
but just look at those crumbs in her silverware draw-
ers!"

Maybe the ultimate force in my life is the desire
to earn the epitaph SHE DIDN'T MAKE DIRT. Anyhow,
by the time I get to my vacation spot, I really need the
rest.

On that trip, we rested. We also settled something
without quite discussing it. I guess it was sunshine
sprinkling through the trees that made Lloyd mellow.
It set him to dreaming. As he awakened from a smiling
sleep, he murmured, "Must see about getting Jinxie's
eyes fixed. Poor Jinxie's all glassy-eyed."

When we returned home I called the vet. I had a new vet now, the young woman with the mobile unit, who had turned out to be very pleasant. She specialized in dogs and cats. And she made house calls. That settled it. I just couldn't see myself chauffeuring four animals, singly or together, to our other vet's office. Baron loathed the place, Barney was his usual neurotic self, and the kittens had traveled in a car only once before. Since the advent of the kittens, I'd been phoning this new vet for advice and moral support. Now I summoned her to inoculate the kittens and inspect the entire menagerie, and I considered her five-dollar house-call fee a bargain.

She is a good vet. She picked up the kittens, stroked and admired them, and immediately gave me two diagnoses. Jesse was not a male. Amazed but flexible, I instantly dubbed her Jessica, and that name stuck. Jinxie's glassy-eyed look was attributed to a condition called conjunctivitis, a congenital ailment. I'd need to put a dab of salve directly onto the eyeball twice daily. Also, she was missing a bit of tail, as a result of Jessica's unruliness. Another tube of salve was supplied.

After all the shots and examinations were given, we sat down at the kitchen table and, over orange juice, discussed the general state of the zoo. Baron was showing his age. Those raw, angry sores were caused by his sedentary lifestyle. Best give him a good, thick mat to lie on. He hardly got up anymore, except to relieve himself, and occasionally to take a sniff at one of the kittens or a bite at Barney.

The vet had, in her gentle, expert manner, knelt down beside Baron and begun to feel his abdomen. He must have sensed her skill, for he abandoned himself utterly to the examination, letting go his usual defenses. He rolled over on his back with a long moan, and his bloodshot eyes entreated, "Oh, doc, I'm sure glad you're here—what can you do for these old bones?"

There was nothing to do. With care, he could survive another year or so. Then his kidneys would give out, or his heart, or the swellings she felt might develop into fatal tumors. But, for the time being, he seemed content enough, accepting his physical limitations and our abundant love.

As for Barney, his problems were obvious. From the moment the vet—and her young assistant—had arrived, Barney made a complete, yapping nuisance of himself. He chased the kittens, stole garbage out of the pail, staged mock attacks on the vet, and tried to mount her assistant, a shy, pretty blonde dressed in faded jeans. (I had noticed something about Barney: young girls, especially blondes wearing jeans, always drove him wild.)

The vet commiserated with me about Barney's

behavior She suggested I take him to school. School? I laughed. Hadn't I enough to do? I'd always trained my dogs without help. She recommended several books. One was written by a dog psychiatrist. She wasn't kidding, and neither was the author. He gets thirty-five dollars for an hour's consultation, during which the entire family is observed *interacting* with the pet. Believe it. I've spoken to this man on the phone. He is very nice. He is also very wealthy. You can tell by his voice.

The vet offered to lend me the book. I accepted. Also, she said that the kittens, at the age of four months, could start sleeping outdoors.

Ah, ecstasy! I would get my den back. But it was Lloyd who balked. Oh, he wanted them outside, but he began to worry, because by this time Jessica had worked her wanton charms on him.

Each night when he came home from work, Jessica would rush to the door, tail held high in expectation, sashay up to rub against his legs, then throw herself down on her back and shimmy from side to side, purring lasciviously and making such an outrageous display that I thought he'd see right through it. But, of course, he didn't. He was—and still is—absolutely convinced that Jessica is madly in love with him.

Well, perhaps she is. But I happen to think she

also knows which side her bread is buttered on. The things she makes him do for her! (Clever female, to know that that's how a man's love is sustained.) She'll sleep soundly on his stomach so he can't move a muscle for hours. She'll leap straight into the tub when he's bathing, nearly scalding herself to death, then need to be rubbed and dried and pampered. At night she'll perch in terror on the roof, crying and wailing, waiting for him to come to the rescue with flashlight and ladder, and he will not believe that all day she scales and descends that same roof without giving it a second thought. If I tell him to ignore her, he says I'm heartless.

Wasn't it too heartless, he wondered, to suddenly put them out at night?

No, no. They probably hated being cooped up in the den, I told him.

Other cats—bad characters—would teach them all sorts of evil tricks, pick fights, and give them fleas, Lloyd claimed.

Oh, they were strong and would protect each other, I countered. As for fleas, they had plenty of their own, not to worry about a few more.

But wouldn't they run away? Wouldn't they feel abandoned? Did I think they would cry out there?

I assured him that they would love sleeping out

all night. I reminded him how our kids used to beg to take their sleeping bags out to the yard. I promised to fix them scrambled eggs in the morning.

"The kittens don't have a sleeping bag," he said. "They don't have *any* beds."

So the next day we got a large wooden box, outfitted it with an old piece of rug and a torn-up fuzzy sweater, and the following week my mother donated a very small doghouse that her poodle had never used. We placed the little doghouse on top of the box, creating a two-story affair. Now, when visitors gaze out the window to the deck below and wonder what that contraption is, I tell them without cracking a smile, "Oh, I'm sure you've heard of them. It's a cathouse."

11

R E C E N T L Y S H A R I posed this question: "If Jinxie were human, what profession do you think she'd have?"

"Librarian," I answered without hesitation. "She'd be a very good and fussy librarian."

Shari agreed. Then we discussed Jessica. "Oh, she'd be a singer," I said, "a buxom woman singing bawdy songs in some rollicking pub. And if any man tried to make a pass at her, she'd flatten him out fast."

Yes, from the start the two were entirely different. It shows that environment is only part of the story when it comes to trying to explain behavior or disposition. Some unexplainable essence also creates distinctions.

I had assumed that the kittens were twins. Later I learned that kittens of the same litter do not necessarily share the same father; sometimes each offspring is sired by a different tom. This, then, explained their physical differences.

Jinx is long and thin, with a small head. Her undershot jaw and slender neck give her the regal look one sees in those Egyptian statues of cats. Her gray coat is sleek and short, with a few calico patches. She has slanted, green-gray eyes that nearly blend into her small face, and coarse gray lashes that are so prominent they look like they were painted on with a fine brush.

Jinxie is a mincing little lady, at best an Abyssinian princess, at times a pessimist, contemplating the worries of the world from the upstairs window, her head hanging low, the picture of depression, meowing pitifully if she thinks herself alone and abandoned.

One might consider Jinx fainthearted, except that she also possesses an overwhelming curiosity. Strangers in the house can terrify her; still, she'll stretch out her body to an incredible extent while peering around corners just to get a whiff of what's going on.

With nose and whiskers she investigates the toilet bowl, the suds in the sink, the fish in its bowl, and, most certainly, all the cupboards in the house. It was Jinxie who discovered the false panel behind the bar and disappeared for hours. Her curiosity also led her deep into the bowels of the washing machine, where she lay under a pile of dirty laundry. She must have used up one of her nine lives that day. I came within a hair's-breadth of turning on the machine, when some inner nudge caused me to check under the lid.

For all her curiosity, Jinx does not venture far from home. She is like a timid little child, darting out to catch some glimpses of the world, then rushing back to mamma's protection. Her protector, often, is Jessica.

Jessica, on the other hand, is self-sufficient and sassy, a splendid specimen of her species. I vote her Most Likely to Survive. She excels at all those important cat skills like running, leaping, scratching, and jumping.

Jessica is a realist. She sizes up a situation and acts upon it—fast. If she wants to escape the dogs— or simply for practice—she claws her way up the draperies and does a tightrope act on the rods. She scales the screen door all the way up to the rafters of our high-beamed ceiling and lies there grinning down at Baron and Barney like Alice's Cheshire cat. (She even resembles her physically.)

Jessica's fur is a tumble of tiger stripes ranging

from white to darkest gray. She has a soft, fluffy white chest and belly, and her eyes are a sparkling green.

She's the typical domestic short-hair pictured on boxes of cat food. Of course, she is far prettier than those commercial types. Our Jessica, with her pink nose and huge eyes, is exceptional. Secretly I call her Nefertiti, which means "The Beautiful One Has Come," because the designation "domestic short-hair" seems so common.

Jessica's ruff is full and her neck is short. When she lies down she reminds me of a maned lion or a smug, double-chinned matriarch. She has a strange way of puffing herself up and making herself so much rounder and fatter that she resembles a pincushion cat.

She is neither shy nor ladylike. Pick her up against her will and she'll scold you with a sharp "Nyech!" Catch her cozily sleeping under forbidden quilts, and she'll glare in outrage and deliver a three-syllable harangue: *"Rech-meach-reh!"*

If we invite anybody into the house, even a repairman, Jessica will disappear, returning late at night if we're lucky. You can't cross Jessica. She's the boss. She's Top Cat.

Her status as Top Cat was established when the kittens were weaned. Jessica was first out of the box, first over the barricade, first to stalk insects and butterflies in the grass. I assume she sometimes catches things —lizards, moths, maybe even small mice. While Jessica stalks, Jinx watches. *Her* prey is a little white pom-pom that was once attached to a bedspread. She'll give that pom-pom a good run for its money anyday.

Jinx, however, was first to use the litter box and to bury her leavings properly. To this day, Jessica can't be bothered to do it right. She'll make a few random scratches, as often as not scratching the linoleum rather than the litter. Then she rushes off to some new adventure, leaving Jinx to tidy up. Jinx does a meticulous job of it.

But ultimately it is at the feeding dish that dominance is established and maintained. Nature demands order. In any animal society, even if it has only two members, hierarchy is essential for survival. Within a week of being weaned, the issue was settled atop our kitchen counter, where the kittens were taking their dinner from two separate dishes.

Jessica, an exuberant eater, devoured her portion and immediately looked around for more. With head lowered truculently, she began to move in on Jinx. Jessica's gait and expression were reminiscent of those teen-age thugs who swagger about in leather jackets.

"Step aside," her manner implied. "I'm taking over."

Jinx withdrew, as astonished as an innocent damsel in a melodrama. Disbelieving, she glanced over her shoulder and then edged her way back toward her dish.

Jessica gave her that fixed stare, daring her.

Pretending that nothing had happened, Jinx casually wandered around to the other side of the dish. In a flash, Jessica's paw struck her flat on the head, and held her there, bound. Jessica's eyes glared her message: "I choose what I will eat, when, how much, and where. I am Top Cat, and don't you ever forget it."

It is a credit to cats that they do not hold grudges. Jinxie lingered but a moment longer, depressed, then saved face by scampering off to sit in the sun and give herself a vigorous washing. She understood nature's requirements. Later, she would return to nibble the crumbs that had fallen over the side of the dish. Later, too, I would slip her something extra, but I would not interfere in their business. It had to be so. Jessica was simply assuming the role for which she was suited, claiming the privileges that went with Top Cat responsibilities.

Responsibilities? Yes, in a cat society there is much to do. Safe, comfortable sleeping places must be established and new ones continually discovered. When strangers come, someone must lead the retreat. When it rains, someone must find a dry lair. Someone must scout to find out whether it's safe to play in the neighbors' yard, and someone must lead the battle when other animals threaten.

Occasionally the neighbors' enormous orange tomcat comes over, attempting to socialize. He sits pressed against the patio window, grinning, cajoling the girls with his whole demeanor: "Come on out, honey, I'll show ya a real good time."

If Jinxie sees him first, she'll hold him off with a glare, a crouch, and several swift swats of her tail—all behind the patio window, of course, and only until Jessica arrives. Then Jinx disappears, leaving Top Cat to finish him off with a series of growls and other threats.

It is the job of Top Cat to keep ever alert, even during sleep. Often I come upon the two of them entwined in slumber on my favorite chair. Jinx is sprawled out with her head thrown back, utterly comatose, while Jessica sleeps with ears twitching, and her eyes will open at the slightest noise. Even if she appears to be sound asleep, her tail occasionally will flip, indicating that she is definitely still on duty. If danger should approach in the form of big dogs or flitting moths or people who might start dragging cats around, she'll warn Jinxie and they'll be off in an instant.

In only one area does Jinxie take the lead: food procurement. When the cats are hungry, it is Jinx who comes to complain, and it has been so from the time they were five weeks old.

Along about dinnertime, Jinx appears in the kitchen and begins her routine. "Meow. Meow!" I look down at her. She runs to the refrigerator and sits down expectantly. I open the door and she peers inside, deciding: hum, what about that tuna left over from lunch? How about some milk? A hamburger?

If I proceed insensitively with preparations for my own dinner, Jinx will sit at my feet and begin ever so gently to pat my ankle. Pat-pat ("Hey, it's me. Dinnertime. Fix it!").

I open a can. Jinxie jumps up to the counter and circles the electric can opener like a worker bee seeking his queen. She sniffs. "What? String beans!" She jumps down, tail flicking angrily.

The vet has told me to give the cats balanced meals, and that means at least fifty percent of their diet should be dry kibble. Cats cannot live on protein alone.

Conscientiously, I set out the kibble. I mix in a little canned cat food, something called seafood salmagundi.

Jinxie sniffs at the offering. Nix. Jessica begins

to pace—round and round, round and round. Somehow, they communicate. "Tell her! Tell her we don't like it!" Jessica tells Jinxie.

Jinx approaches my ankle again. Pat. Pat-pat. Then she rises on her hind legs and pats again. "Nice," she is saying. "We want nice. You know. How about that old piece of chicken liver you guys don't want anyhow?"

Okay. So, they win. I put aside the salad I'm fixing. I haul out the tidbits. So, they like to have good things to eat. Who can blame them? We don't really need chopped chicken liver for hors d'oeuvres. Too much cholesterol.

12

I T W A S S U M M E R , and Lloyd and I were out hiking all alone. No kids, no pets, just the two of us—ah, bliss. As we tramped across the scrubby hillsides, we talked, and the conversation soon focused on how wonderful it was to be off by ourselves like this.

No sooner had we thus begun to count our blessings than we quickly progressed to counting our worries, which sprang from the very fact that neither of the kids was with us. Dan had gone off backpacking and mountain climbing to some undisclosed and probably snake-infested destination. Shari was spending the day at one of those marathon rock concerts, which I had approved several weeks earlier while I was obviously not in my right mind.

It was a bad situation. While we plodded through the underbrush, Lloyd and I conjured up a whole host of deranged criminals, mechanical failures, and natural disasters, any one of which might overtake either of our children at any moment.

We soon realized that we were on a real worry binge, and this led, naturally, to problem solving. What we needed was a target. A scapegoat. Here we were, feeling awful on a perfectly fine day. Why? Because we were overtired, oppressed by responsibilities, overextended. One thing led to another. Soon we were vigorously climbing a rather steep hill, caught up in the full heat of discussion, and the subject was Barney: his faults.

At last. We had come to the very source of our problems—Barney.

As in any analysis, we began with a case history. Barney had been with us for nine months. That was certainly sufficient time in which to assess his personality and adjustment. We zeroed in on him like two parole officers making out their report. We labeled him unruly, hyperactive, and undisciplined. He had no conscience, did not care what others thought of him, concerned himself only with the utmost foolishness, and seemed bent on destroying everything in his path.

We did not stay long on such generalities; we elaborated with actual examples. Barney still jumped on people. Shari's girl friends could never pass through our patio gate without being subjected to Barney's assaults. He also leaped at old ladies (my mother). Oh, if a pregnant woman should ever come through our gate . . . We shuddered.

Barney would never lie still and watch TV like a respectable dog. He insisted upon slobbering and pacing, soliciting strokes, pawing at us, groveling, climbing onto the sofa. If someone's hand hung down over the side of a chair, Barney would grab it in his mouth and guide it to his tummy.

When passing through a room, Barney would snatch up anything portable, including small radios, hair brushes, shoes, clothes, and always the *TV Guide*.

There was obviously something wrong with that dog—upstairs. He was either educationally handicapped or mentally deficient. It had taken a full four months to train him to relieve himself any place but in our patio. He still ran the other way when he was called, and he had taken to chasing cars. He didn't seem to care what we thought of him. No amount of discussion, or explanation, scolding, or swatting on the rump with newspapers did any good whatsoever. And worst of all the nightly bedtime fuss.

At bedtime, we'd first have to corner him, which took a number of turns around the yard, then get him captured inside the house. From there it was upstairs and downstairs, until coaxing gave way to screaming, and Barney was finally dragged into the garage and the door slammed behind him.

Like proper prosecuting attorneys, we made our summation as we descended the hill and walked, slowly now, back home. Barney was not a good pal, a faithful watchdog, or a valued asset to our family. He was a misfit. For whatever reason, physical, emotional, or psychological, he was incorrigible. We had tried to mold him, reform him, rehabilitate him. All in vain. Only one reasonable solution remained.

We decided, then and there, to get rid of Barney.

"I feel," said Lloyd solemnly, "as if a great weight has been lifted from my shoulders."

We sauntered along in an almost dreamy state, holding hands, making plans.

"I'll be able to go out into the backyard again anytime I want," Lloyd murmured. "I'll be able to lie out in the patio, maybe even cook hamburgers on the barbecue again. . . ."

"There's still time to put in some zinnias for summer," I mused.

A whole world of possibilities opened before us. Friends could come to visit us again without trauma. I could have uninterrupted conversations on the phone again. The kitchen floor would shine again. I'd be able to make it directly from the car into the house with my grocery bags again, without having to pay for my folly with a half-hour chase through the neighborhood.

The rest of the afternoon passed in a haze of contentment. In our minds, Barney was already gone, and our days were filled with pleasant activities and long, long periods of tranquillity.

That night, as we dragged Barney to bed, bribing him with "cookies," Lloyd said cheerfully, "Well, this might be your last night, old boy."

Tomorrow I was to start making inquiries about a good home for Barney. Tomorrow, too, I'd tell the children of our decision. They might put up a token resistance, but they too were thoroughly exasperated with Barney. Besides, when children see that their parents are firm, they tend to comply.

As I got into the shower and then settled down for the night, I felt almost numb, like a person who has endured some long ordeal that is finally over. My thoughts centered on visions of a home for Barney, and finally crystallized into one particular scenario.

It would be a nice home, a lovely home. Yes, even a better home than ours, with a mamma who was sweet-tempered and cheerful, who only smiled and nodded when dogs stole her rice pudding or dug up her roses. You know, one of those hardy, frontier types described in stories: "Brimming with warmth and good humor, she smiled fondly at her little ones and drew them unto her ample bosom . . ." They always have that ample bosom.

Yes, I'd find a good home, where the dad was a real pal, the kind who'd just tousle a boy's hair instead of yelling when the toilet overflowed because the kid had flushed a Tinkertoy down it. The kind who'd go for long hikes in the wilderness with the noble dog beside him. The sort of man whose car never had sticky door handles or doggie-nose prints on the side windows. Or if it did, he never noticed.

That perfect family would have children, of course, preferably boys. Preferably two or three or ten little boys, all of whom would love nothing better than to play with Barney day and night. It ought, furthermore, to be a poor family, one with few material possessions, certainly not a stereo, carpets, TV, or books. In fact, a family whose abode was a nearly furnitureless shack with dirt floors and no amenities, where children and animals flopped indiscriminately onto bunks, ate hamburgers together from a common plate, and no one ever bothered to clean at all.

Such a family would lavish love on our Barney. This delightful group of happy, wholesome American children would transform Barney into friend-follower-protector, that canine stereotype envisioned by nearly every mythmaker this country has ever known.

All I had to do tomorrow was find this family.

13

FOR TWO DAYS I didn't call my mother. She would have asked me, "So, what's new?"

I would have had to tell her, "We're thinking of getting rid of Barney."

She'd interrogate me. "What do you mean? You'll sell him? Give him away? Abandon him? Are you serious? Are you crazy?"

So, I didn't call her. Instead, I asked myself all the questions she would have asked, then proceeded to answer them, engaging myself in an endless inner dialogue. I was strong and rational. It was downright irrational to keep a dog that didn't fit in with the family. Just because we'd made a mistake, did that mean we had to suffer for it for the next ten years or so? Lots of people give away dogs. People even give away *people*. Ever heard of divorce? Why couldn't we just divorce that dog?

Certain dogs and certain families, I persisted, are temperamentally incompatible. Probably everyone has, at one time or another, gotten rid of an unsuitable pet. Mentally I collected data on everyone I knew who had given away a dog. This list included some pretty respectable people—it even included my own mother. Still, I felt guilty and defensive. I had to restrain myself from approaching strangers in the supermarket to inquire, "Excuse me, but have you ever given away a dog?"

I began to imagine Barney's transfer. Would it be for money? No, no, too crass. I tried to envision giving him to a neighbor's cleaning lady. Within a week she would be so totally fed up that she'd pass him on to her cousin, who in turn would pawn him off on his brother-in-law, a black-hearted lout who would either beat him or sell him to some laboratory where crazed scientists would perform vile experiments on him without benefit of anesthetic.

I became edgy. Edgy? Fit to be tied was more like it. Several times during the day I would look at Barney and burst into tears.

Lloyd, meanwhile, went around the house with an attitude of contentment bordering on sheer joy. Occasionally he alluded to Barney's departure, to be achieved "within a day or so." He had left the details to me.

Once or twice he gave me a sidelong, quizzical glance and asked, "Barney's still leaving, right?"

I nodded. "Yes, as soon as I find him a good home. I'm working on it."

I slept, but with visions of poor Barney abused by a hundred different owners, until truly vicious from lack of love, he had to be locked in a cage. I envisioned his face, that black pointed nose, those rolling eyes, his lovely golden ruff, his long tongue licking my cheek as I said goodbye. Throughout the vision I also had the nagging certainty that Barney would leave us without a backward glance. In reality, dogs are not usually as faithful as Lassie.

Well, I had made a decision, and, true to my intention, I telephoned Mrs. Fritz, who lived around the corner. The Fritzes had lost their dog several weeks earlier. They suspected he'd been poisoned. Were they looking for another dog?

Perhaps they were, Mrs. Fritz said cautiously.

Might they be interested in Barney?

Why would we ask? Weren't we happy with Barney?

Oh, certainly, we were happy with Barney—happy as could be. The trouble was, Baron didn't get along with him. That was it. Baron just couldn't adjust to us having another dog in the house. And it didn't seem quite fair to force him. Now, Barney was a very beautiful dog, and he even had papers, and if we could find a good home for him, perhaps we could be persuaded . . .

Mrs. Fritz said she'd think about it and let me know.

I figured the deal was no deal. I telephoned my friend Madge, who was moving to a lovely, pastoral community some hundred miles south of us. Madge was a good mother, a wonderful wife, and an animal lover.

I made my voice sound cheerful as I spoke to her. "We just can't keep Barney," I explained, "because of poor Baron. Would you like to have him? You could take him to your new home."

Rather sharply Madge declined. She told me that she had just had a tooth pulled, their gardener had sprayed the wrong trees, and she couldn't possibly take Barney with her.

I was back at square one. I checked the newspapers. Nobody was looking for a year-old German shepherd who had no manners. Ought I to advertise, then? No. No telling what sort of people might turn up. Deep in my heart I harbored the suspicion that some people sell dogs, like old horses, to glue factories.

Meanwhile, I was developing all the symptoms of Emotional Crisis—forgetting where I'd put things; burning the onions for our stew, twice; stumbling into the counters and chairs; snapping at people. And in the shower, instead of showering, I was crying.

Our fateful hike had taken place on a Saturday. By Monday night I was a wreck. By Tuesday I had chills and took my temperature four times. Then, as I was taking Barney and Baron for their afternoon walk, with Barney tugging away at the leash like a locomotive, I remembered something. There was another solution. It was drastic, to be sure, but these were critical times.

I ran home to call the YMCA. I had heard about their obedience training classes for dogs but had dismissed the idea. Too much fuss. Too far to travel. And I'd be hanged if I'd have some wise-guy instructor trying to tell me how to train my dog!

I quickly dialed the number and, despite my resolve to speak calmly and dispassionately, I began to blubber out my story.

"We're about to give him away! I don't want to

part with my dog, but he's so awful, so undisciplined. He's hyperactive," I babbled, "since we got him from a kennel where he didn't get enough attention or human love, and even though the vet said it might be possible . . ."

The woman on the other end of the line had obviously been through this sort of thing before. She said, "It sounds as though your dog is unusually difficult to train."

"Yes! Yes!" And to convince her that I was blameless, I began to tell her about the many dogs I'd owned since I was ten, how I'd trained every one of them, how my Skippy had done twelve different tricks, his tour de force being a mock tightrope act done on a suspended plank. I ended by telling her about Baron, whom we had housebroken in three days flat and who always conducted himself with gentlemanly deportment.

"I can see that you have a problem," she said. "From what you tell me, Barney might not be as sound of temperament as you would wish, but you've naturally become attached to him, and you want to explore every possible avenue. . . ."

"Yes! Yes!" I cried, my heart racing. She understood! I pictured a study, frontier type, ample bosom and all.

"So it would seem that obedience training could be

the answer. It might be his last hope."

Now it was her turn to speak at length, while I listened with the fervor of a remorseful sinner getting the gospel.

Yes, there was hope for Barney, she said. She had trained hundreds, thousands of dogs, some of whose owners had already considered having them "put down." With obedience training a dog could gain self-control and self-respect. His entire disposition could undergo a beneficial change. I, she assured me, was being a good citizen in seeking obedience training. My dog, would, in turn, become a better citizen. Certainly there was little to lose and much to gain. "Think of it," she said, "as his last reprieve."

How much would this reprieve cost me?

A mere twenty-six dollars. And twenty hours of my time—two hours each Saturday afternoon for the next ten weeks. Luckily for me, a new class was beginning the very next Saturday. She would sign us up immediately.

I nearly swooned with relief. "He jumps up on people," I offered, thinking, perhaps, to test her.

"That's easy to correct. Knock him down."

"He runs away!"

"We'll fix that in class."

For each canine crime, this woman, whose name

was Lois, had a ready response. And she instructed me sternly, "You must immediately stop comparing Barney to Baron."

I promised to obey.

"And no roughhousing with the dog!"

I agreed.

"Think of it," she repeated, "as his last reprieve."

I did.

14

T H E K I D S W E R E not at all surprised to learn that I'd changed my mind. That's because I'm so consistent. Consistently wishywashy. I'm not sure who bet whom what, but I think some money did pass hands between my children and their pals, and a friend of my daughter's told me calmly, "We all knew you wouldn't give Barney away."

Lloyd did not ask any questions, make any declarations, or shoot any sly glances my way. In a good marriage, one essential ingredient is an occasional stretch of total noncommunication, in which more is communicated than at any other time.

Some months earlier, Lloyd had purchased a book on obedience training written by an acknowledged expert. I had browsed through it at the time and dismissed its methods as being too stern. Now I began to read avidly.

From the moment I had hung up the phone after talking with Lois, I was filled with energy and resolve. I'd make a citizen out of Barney or collapse in the attempt. Thus, I began to educate myself, the better to educate my dog.

Even from my brief conversation with Lois, I could tell that her methods were the same as those of the author of the book Lloyd had bought. In essence, real obedience training demands a consistently firm, authoritarian approach; the human, not the dog, is boss.

I later learned that both the book and Lois used the standard method accepted by the American Kennel Club. Basically, the dog is taught to obey these commands: heel, sit, sit-stay, down, down-stay, and come. Everything else is variation or window dressing. The result is not only mastery of these commands but greater emotional stability.

The book was addressed to those dog owners of

weak will and cringing attitude who let their dogs get away with murder, deluding themselves that time will cure a scoundrel or that kindess and patience will cure an animal's sheer cussedness. In short, the author was addressing this entire volume to *me*.

As I read, I blushed and sighed and resolved to change my ways. Then I went out to the patio where Barney was snapping at flies, and I told him the way it was going to be.

"Barney, this is it. You must reform. If you are to stay with us, you must become a decent and respectable dog. I can no longer put up with your antics, bad manners, and your dangerous and disgusting behavior."

We had an old chain choke collar lying around. I slipped it around Barney's neck and snapped on the leash. "Now," I said firmly, "we are going to have lesson number one." I couldn't bear to wait until Saturday. Barney's training would begin immediately, the better to prepare him for that first class.

I walked. He balked. I tugged. He turned. It went on for half an hour. When it was over, Barney seemed strangely subdued and tired.

The lessons continued for the next four days, half an hour a day, as the book prescribed. In addition to training him to heel, I began really watching his bad behavior instead of trying to ignore it. He began chewing on Shari's purse. I gave him a sharp rap on the mouth. He snapped up a kitchen towel. Instead of giving chase, I marched straight up to him and let him have it again. He released the towel immediately and slunk away. I was beginning to get through to him.

Barney began to watch me in a different way. He'd lie by the kitchen door, his eyes upon me, probably thinking, "What in the world's gotten into the old gal? I think she really means it!"

I kept after that dog for the next four days like a drill sergeant with his troops. I didn't let him get away with anything. I stopped pretending that I hadn't really called him or that I hadn't told him to stay out. I said what I meant and meant what I said, and on the third night Lloyd ventured a question.

"What's gotten into Barney?"

He was, for the first time in his life, lying quietly on the kitchen floor, not bothering anyone.

"I guess he's made a decision," I said obliquely, unwilling to tout my success, particularly since we hadn't even begun school yet.

By Saturday I was excited. I was ready in plenty of time—for a change—and arrived at the Y about ten minutes early. Barney absolutely loved the ride over. He was being so good that I began to wonder whether he really needed the class after all.

I let him out of the car and snapped on the leash. Barney walked a few steps with me. Then he took a look at all those other dogs waiting for the teacher, and he made such a mighty, whiplash lunge that I felt as if my arms were being yanked out of their sockets.

But I hung on for dear life, dimly aware that some twenty dogs and their owners were watching, and I said farewell to dignity at the YMCA.

Somehow I coaxed Barney back to the side of the building, where he wouldn't have to see the other dogs. We crouched there until the instructor arrived, and the moment I laid eyes on her I knew I was outclassed. She was terrific. She was everything I'm not, and exactly what it takes to be a dog trainer.

She was tall and robust, and her very walk conveyed relentless determination and infinite calm. The lines about her mouth, the firmness of her chin, boasted "no nonsense." And her outfit—it was superbly tailored to her task. A man's shirt of faded pink-and-gray plaid hung out over pants of a nondescript color, probably tan, which were caught up at the ankles and stuffed into boots and so fuzzed up, limp and lint-laden that they seemed to be left over from the last millennium.

Her hair was piled into a sort of doughnut shape on the top of her head, and her eyes were keen. She took us all in—dogs and people—and she knew exactly all our foibles, all our problems, and self-delusions.

At first she said not a word, but motioned with both hands for us to move into a circle. One hand was ominously bandaged. I felt certain that her antagonist —man or beast—had had the worst of the encounter.

Now she boomed out her introduction. "This class in dog obedience is designed to make your dog a better citizen, more acceptable to others, and happier with himself. You will learn how to control your dog, and the dog will be given a constructive outlet for his energy."

At this, a basset hound let out a terrible howl. Lois totally ignored him.

"This course is approved by the ASPCA and the American Humane Society. There is only one instructor here, and I am that instructor. These dogs are going to learn self-control. They are going to learn manners. They are going to learn . . ."

A mixed-breed husky began to bark at a boxer. Lois raced over to the offender and inquired of his owner, "Why are you allowing your dog to threaten that boxer?"

"He's afraid of him," murmured the owner, a thin little woman. "Maybe he's protecting me."

"What's there to be afraid of? I'm not afraid of that boxer. Nobody else is afraid of that boxer. Don't let your dog threaten other dogs like that. This is a public place. This is a group meeting. Your dog need not protect you against anybody at the YMCA."

Our motley group, both dogs and people, seemed

to straighten up as one, and as one we fell silent.

"I will have no dogfights here!" Lois declared, once again the center of the ring. She whipped out a piece of rubber hose from somewhere, then tossed it smartly into the ring so that we all might see it and marvel. "If your dog gets into a fight with another dog," she shouted, "I will whack him over the head with this rubber hose! If your dog growls at another person or starts to bite," she shouted, "I will whack him over the head with this rubber hose!"

She attempted a moment of levity, one of very few during the entire length of the course: "If after four of five weeks you are still letting your dog get away with bad behavior," she was still yelling, "I'll whack *you* over the head with this rubber hose!"

The jest was lost on her gaping, gasping audience. I glanced around. Oh, what an assemblage! Big dogs, little dogs, dogs with spots and dogs with curls, shaggy dogs, low-slung dachshunds, a spider-legged whippet, an enormous Great Dane, two Labrador puppies who kept getting tangled up in each other, the poodles in their variety, and the variety dogs with their masters and mistresses, teen-age boys, stout young matrons, an elderly gentleman, a woman wearing a suede suit and gold necklaces, a young married couple, a tight-lipped executive, a burly, tough-looking fellow—and me.

"We will begin! Make a circle!" Lois yelled. Then she began to chant in a loud singsong: "We are going to condition this dog. This is going to be a working dog. This dog is now working for YOU."

She grabbed a leash and took hold of an unsuspecting dalmation to demonstrate. "What's his name? 'Yank?' All right, Yank, heel!"

She showed us how. It looked easy. Now all we had to do was to step briskly around in a circle.

"Barney, heel!"

Forward we rushed, pulling and tripping, and then Lois would shout, "About face!" which sent everyone into a tangle and a mad scramble for position.

How long did it last? I had no way of knowing. I only knew that eventually I was covered with sweat, my arms and shoulders ached, and my hair stood frizzily on end.

Only once did the teacher notice me. "Good-looking shepherd," she said. My mouth was too dry to respond. I tried to smile and managed a grimace. She added, "Step it up! Keep pace! Give him a good *jerk!*"

At last she said blithely, "Class, go sit down with your dogs on the curb over there in the shade."

I gazed at that strip of shade, incredulous. No way, I thought, would these twenty odd crazy animals sit there with their masters. No way. But they did.

They sat there, large and little, floppy and smooth, they sat there all in a row in the shade, with their owners meekly beside them, and Lois declared with a smile, "These dogs are already fifty percent better than they were two hours ago."

She bade us goodbye with the admonition that was to become custom: "Practice! If you are satisfied with your dog's progress, you just aren't expecting enough!"

I made my way home, exhausted, dazed, and awed. Once I glanced around at Barney in the back seat, where he had utterly collapsed. I could see we shared exactly the same emotions.

15

I WALKED INTO the house nonchalantly, told Barney, "Lie down," took off his leash, and got myself a cold soda pop. Dan, Shari, and Lloyd stood there gaping.

"What's the matter with Barney?"

"Did the teacher whip him?

"Is he sick? Did they hurt him?"

"Has he already *learned?*"

I replied coolly, "Barney is tired from his lesson. He didn't rush in the door ahead of me and he didn't try to trip me or tear apart the screen door because he is now a scholar and a citizen, and that is a full-time job. Shari, you've got to stop screaming and waving your arms at him. Lloyd, you cannot play tug-of-war with the dog or let him jump on you. He is in *training*."

"Like a football player!" Shari exclaimed.

"Oh, what a good dog," Dan said, beaming.

"Tell us," Lloyd demanded, and I took center stage in the middle of the kitchen, where I acted out every part—the domineering teacher with her rubber hose, the cowardly poodle, the angry Doberman, the dressed-up lady with her Great Dane, the stubborn boxer, the sheep dog wearing pink barrettes to keep the hair out of his eyes, and, of course, Barney.

"What did the teacher say about Barney?"

"Was he the worst in the class?"

"Was he the best?"

"He was—just about average. . . . Maybe," I reluctantly admitted, "a little worse than average. He was," I sighed, "the only one who actually ran away."

Then I had to go over it all, and I hammed it up, and they responded like Gilbert and Sullivan fans, and all three of them begged to accompany me the next time.

"We'll see," I said with a sniff. "After all, this is no game. It's serious business."

I worked with Barney every day for a half hour or more. In between training periods I virtually ignored him, as Lois had suggested. Each training period ended with success and praise. And I automatically began taking Barney with me when I went out in the car. People got used to seeing me with him at the shopping center, I guess. At first we must have made quite a spectacle: Barney, in his terror, pulling away from every person and every strange object. The sight of a pillar made him shiver; the automatic doors at the bank threw him into a panic. But one day I got him through those doors and up to the teller's window, where I told him, "Sit," and, by golly, he obeyed.

The teller was impressed. "I could never take my dog out like that," she said admiringly.

The family could hardly believe it when I told them Barney had been to the bank. I enlarged upon that experience by including the laundry and the beauty-supply store among his regular haunts. I'm not saying he's now perfectly well adapted to strangers. He still refuses to associate with the clerk at the paint store. An odd object, like an electric fan or a barrel, will send him into spasms. But self-control is a relative matter, and the learning of it is very gradual.

Things also began to improve at home. Occasionally Barney came when he was called. At least he began to recognize the difference between right and wrong. It had baffled me before that he never responded to his own naughtiness with any sense of remorse. Now, if I caught him chewing something, he'd run into the corner, tail pressed between his legs, fully expecting punishment. Sometimes a mere look or a word helped him to resist temptation. He began, in short, to exhibit signs of having a conscience, or at least a sense of cause and effect.

Now, when Lloyd came home from work, he could, by the simple expedient of commanding, "Stay!" cross the patio without getting his suit shredded. At night, with the help of the leash and the command "Heel!", we'd get Barney into the garage.

Sometimes I'd hear Dan talking to Barney. "You are a good citizen, Barney. Does the citizen want to go for a ride?"

As I spent more time with Barney I began to view him as more of a companion than a pest. Since the beginning, I had been reluctant to spend time with Barney alone, for fear of making Baron jealous. Now I became more realistic. It made no sense at all to neglect Barney's training because of concern for Baron's feelings. The two dogs were not exactly friends anyway. Baron still got his share of rides and outings. And I had to be practical. It wasn't fair to limit the young dog because of the physical incapacity of the old.

Thus, we made new accommodations.

Don't get the idea that it was smooth or easy. In class there was, naturally, one goody-goody, smart-aleck dog who did everything right, who went through his paces with tail wagging and head high, who was always selected for demonstrations, who made his master proud. Whenever that dog strutted his stuff, Barney would blithely look the other way.

I cannot count the times Barney made a fool of me, breaking away from the group and fleeing the training area, with everybody looking on, laughing, shaking their heads, congratulating themselves for not having the worst dog in class.

When it came to the sit-stay or the down-stay, it was always touch and go, and Lois sometimes gave extra instruction for Barney. "He's an introvert," she would explain to the class, nodding toward my now fully grown shepherd, one hundred pounds of dog traditionally associated with police work and border patrols. Somehow the word *introvert* always left them laughing.

Each Saturday, as I pulled into the parking lot at the YMCA, Barney would crouch in the bottom of the car, edging his way to the opposite door, eyes shut, entreating me in body language, "You go on by yourself this time, okay? I don't wanna go to school!"

121

But go to school we did, every Saturday until graduation. When we graduated, we started over again. Lois had announced tactfully, without mentioning names or looking at anyone in particular, that some people might find it profitable to repeat the course. I knew exactly who she was talking about. I signed up again.

I'd love to be able to say that Barney was at the head of his class the second time around. But it wasn't so. I had, after all, started out with a hypertense, basket case of a dog, a dog I had been ready to give to the lowest bidder. The very fact that he could perform in an average way and that we could *begin* to cope with him was enough. To me, it was even remarkable.

More remarkable was the telephone call from Mrs. Fritz a few weeks after we'd started obedience training. "About Barney," she said excitedly, "can we come over this afternoon? My Janey has been over to see him through the gate a few times. She thinks he's the sweetest, dearest dog she's ever seen. She adores him. And my husband loves German shepherds, and he's seen Barney too. Have you decided on a price? Could we come over this afternoon and take . . . ?"

My mouth went dry. I simply couldn't believe it. Why would anybody want Barney?

I gazed at him lying out there in the patio on his

striped mat, mouthing a tennis ball, tossing it up, re-trieving it, playing by himself like a little kid trying to be good.

"We've decided to—uh—keep Barney," I told Mrs. Fritz. And ever so gently I suggested that if they were going to get a dog from somewhere else, she should be sure to have him checked by an expert—a vet or a trainer—or learn to determine for herself the soundness and temperament of a dog. I explained that several simple tests could be employed to determine whether a dog was too shy or too aggressive, whether he might be friendly toward people, and easily train-able.

She was impressed with my foresight and grateful for my advice. She understood, she said, why we had decided to keep Barney. She could see it wasn't easy to find the right dog, a dog of good breeding and dis-position, one who was also attractive and lovable like our Barney. How very kind we had been even to think of offering him.

I slunk away from the phone, feeling as guilty as Barney looks when he steals a slipper.

16

AFTER A WHILE, in any relationship, the honeymoon is over. That doesn't mean affection is diminished. It merely means that those involved can settle down to the business of living together, secure in the knowledge that responsibilities are divided, idiosyncrasies accepted, and love remains.

So it was for all of us—cats, dogs, and people. We came to a period of truce. Barney and Baron tolerated each other, more or less. Baron lay sedentary on his mat, content to be left alone, while Barney explored his potential.

About the only thing that would get Baron up onto his feet—besides purely physical need—was the sight of Jinx. She was his kitty. If she wandered out to the patio, Baron would stagger up to take a sniff at her and steal a kiss or two.

It was also Jinx who took over the discipline of Barney. If his kisses became too passionate or his pursuit too frantic, she'd leap up on the kitchen table to sit aloof and queenly. Should he dare to show a whisker on that table, Jinx would lash out with sharp claws. Countertops, too, became sacred cat territory, and Jinx was vigilant, sometimes to the point of over-zealousness. Barney could be innocently walking by, and she'd stretch out full length to give him a good swat, just to let him know who's boss.

Jessica, on the other hand, believes in passive resistance. If Barney comes to kiss her, she'll give him that cold, disdainful stare, that flip of the tail implying, "Are you *quite* finished now, Buster? Why don't you just get lost?" Barney, discouraged, then slinks away.

As the cats grew older, I picked up several books on cat behavior. Like those books written for parents of teen-agers, they were good on generalities, lousy when it came to specifics. They explained, for example, that cats like to rub up against things to mark them with their scent. That explained Jinxie's burning desire to examine every single item I'd bring into the house.

It did not, however, explain why both cats leap inside an open box or paper bag, or why they lie down immediately on anything spread out flat, from carbon paper to my best dress to the placemats on the table.

All cat books tell you to provide a scratching post so the cats can keep their claws in shape without ruining your furniture. I provided a scratching post—a big, beautiful carpet-covered extravaganza of a scratching post. Repeatedly I'd sit in front of it, stretching out catlike, making scratching noises with my fingernails. So, what happened? The cats obviously thought that this was *my* scratching post. They continued to use the couch.

The book did explain some of their sounds. To my surprise, I discovered that cats have a large vocabulary. I had thought their vocalizations were limited to "meow" and "ouch." Not so. For many months I continued to hear new sounds from the kittens, beginning with the cheerful "Breep!" which must mean, "Hello there!" or "Thank you very much," as it is given only when we let them in or when we return home after being away for some hours. If they've been out for a long time, or are extremely happy to see us, we may be treated to a series of exclamations—"Brreep! Breep! Meoreep!"

I have also noticed two kinds of growls. One is a

low-throated, deep-bellied, threatening growl, aimed at invading cats from the neighborhood. The other is the whiny, "leave me alone" growl, a milder, more petulant sound reserved for humans.

I have heard both cats click in warning at a bird perched on our patio table. That click-click-click, accompanied by a certain crouch and a rapid switching of the tail, says, "Look out, look out, you idiot bird, I'm gonna getcha!"

In the night we often hear the real knock-down, drag-out territorial-rights screaming of cats, our own and others, and while we sometimes stare out into the darkness with real trepidation, morning proves that it's been mostly a game of bluff, and everyone is fine, the encounters of the night forgotten.

Of meows there are many, the loud forlorn meow, the little hungry meow, the muffled "I'm lost" meow, and even the silent meow made famous by Paul Gallico and his literary feline friend.

Aside from their oral vocabulary, I discovered that cats have a range of body language far more extensive than that of dogs. Their acrobatics put the best of the Russian gymnasts to shame. In every posture and manipulation of tail, cats tell you exactly what they think of you, and often it isn't complimentary.

Cats and dogs are so very different, it's hard to believe that, as some experts claim, they are descended from the same distant ancestors. Why, for instance, can't a cat guard your home? A cat has vicious claws, fangs, and the ability to pounce on the unsuspecting burglar. I can just see it, the printed warning to turn aside the criminal: THIS RESIDENCE IS PROTECTED BY CATS.

Why not? Because cats can't be bothered. Your stuff and your personal welfare are your business. The cat has other things to do.

And that's another thing about cats as compared to dogs. A dog kills time, chewing on a pebble, fooling around with his ball or bone, just waiting for somebody to plan some activity for him. The highlight of his day is a walk, a ride, or getting vacuumed—all activities supplied by humans. Cats, on the other hand, don't sit around waiting for us to devise things to do. Unless they're sleeping or washing, cats are busy making their own plans. You can tell that a cat is always just about to begin a novel or take the clock apart or invent some new weathermaking machine.

Independent? Ha! That isn't the half of it. Try to cuddle a cat that doesn't want loving, and it will let out a "Nyech!" of utter disgust, and then, meaningfully turning its rear toward you, it will begin washing. There is nothing equalitarian in the relationship between a person and a cat. *They* decide when it's time for anything physical between you. The rest of the time—get lost.

So, I go about my business, trying not to offend the cats by forcing myself upon them. I go down to my den, turn on my electric typewriter, and start to work. They allow me to get thoroughly engrossed, at which point Jinxie dashes in with a hearty breep! and leaps onto the table. She takes a few swipes at the pen, she pushes away several loose papers, and sits down on the page I'm copying. If I continue to ignore her, she jumps onto my lap, faces the keys, and watches the motion of the carriage as if it were the movie of the week.

I let her be. I can type with a cat on my lap. But she isn't satisfied. She turns herself around, climbs up my chest until her paws rest on my shoulders, and then she presses her tiny wet nose against the tip of my nose. In case I still haven't gotten her message, she begins to make rhythmic kneading motions with her paws on either side of my neck, in unmistakable anticipation.

What can I do? The animal hungers for affection. I turn off my typewriter. We cuddle.

Next comes Jessica. Her approach is cool. For a long time she sits on the table, giving me the fish-eye. "You," her stare says, "are a selfish person. You do not care about cats. All you care about is working that dumb machine."

She jumps down and stalks out. "I'm leaving. For good."

"Good. Then I can write."

A moment later she returns, leaps up on my chair, and sits behind me so that as I type she can work on my left arm. She swipes at it with her paw, then takes little bites. They tickle. They hurt. They are love bites. I capitulate. All right. I take her onto my lap, cuddle her in my arms. All right, I won't work anymore. What could be more important than this moment and this cat?

Just as I am committed to togetherness, Jessica loses interest. She leaves, and starts, vigorously, to wash, suggesting that my own personal hygiene leaves something to be desired.

In time, the cats settle down to sleep, Jessica, taking over the wooden box where I keep my manuscript, Jinx lying atop one of my slippers, which are under my desk. (I hadn't wanted to mention it, but Jinxie has a shoe fetish. She makes love to my fuzzy pink slippers every chance she gets.)

Wherever they sleep, they leave little deposits of cat hair and flea dirt, those tiny brown specks that turn into bits of blood when touched with water. The first time I saw those specks of blood in the tub (where Jinx had been napping), I phoned the vet in alarm. "Flea droppings," she explained. "Fleas eat blood, so that's what they leave." It made sense. It also made me initiate the daily flea-hunt, during which I usually bag about half a dozen of the creatures. A strange type of daily recreation, perhaps, but the cats have trained me well.

They have taught me many disciplines. Number one is, "Look before you turn anything on." That goes for the dishwasher, the oven, the clothes washer, the automobile, and even the big soup pot. Yes, they have been found sleeping in all of these. Number two is "Hide the goodies." Whatever the books say about feline nutrition, I'm sure most cats would have suggestions of their own. Jinx happens to favor chocolate Oreo cookies. She also likes butter straight from the package, and nuts. Not just any old nuts, mind you, but a special mix of unroasted peanuts, sunflower kernels, and pumpkin seeds, sprinkled with coconut. Jessica, on the other hand, likes a little nip of white wine, a taste of bacon, and she'll devour every trace of a chicken leg before you can say, "Scat!"

People who have never lived with cats probably find it difficult to understand that anyone would allow them to have the run of the house this way. I used to look down on my neighbor for her foolishness and shudder with disgust at the sight of two or three cats writhing around on her dining-room table. The very idea of eating anything at her house turned my stomach. Just how far I have fallen was demonstrated a month or so ago, at Shari's birthday dinner.

I had set the table with a floral centerpiece and the good china, and as we sat around in a festive mood, I was hardly aware of the small intruder trying to nibble a biscuit off my plate. With absentminded little gestures I kept pushing Jinxie aside, still engrossed in lively conversation, until Shari burst out laughing.

"Mother!" she exclaimed. "Do you realize what you're doing? What if I'd told you a year ago that you would be sitting here at the table with a cat on your plate?"

May it serve me as a lesson in judging others.

Now, when it comes to judging others, a certain relative of mine (who shall remain nameless) came for a weekend visit not long ago and became quite agitated during Sunday breakfast, all because Jessica wanted a bit of cream out of the pitcher and Jinxie wished to share the egg yolk on my plate.

She asked a good many questions and voiced a good many opinions about germs and worms and hair balls and things called standards.

Do you know what I'm going to do? For her birthday I'm going to give her a little kitty. Or maybe two. Then she'll see.

17

W E   H A D   A   L O V E L Y summer and a mild fall. And in the secret way that is known only to animals, Baron seemed to foresee a cold, harsh winter. The cold weather got into his joints. He whimpered more often, and sometimes he lay motionless, with a haunted, distant look in his eyes. His coat lost its luster.

Baron would no longer move into the garage at night. He slept on the patio on a thick lounge pad that I had covered with a sheet. The sheet had to be laundered often, for the sores on his elbows bled. As the nights grew longer and colder, I'd cover him with another sheet, and he'd lie in the corner on his pad like a feeble patient, doubtful of the morning.

As I said good night to him, I, too, wondered about the morning: Would he wake? And if he did not, mightn't it be for the best, and merciful?

He was in pain. It hurt him to stand, to lie down, and to walk. No longer could he use his forepaws independently. To get up or down from the curb he had to execute a little hop, and sometimes he fell.

The question had been in my mind for months: What should we do? How long should we avoid deciding and watch the slow, agonizing process of deterioration? With death the inevitable end, must we wait until it became painful beyond bearing?

Then came the responses. What right had we to judge life's rightful length or quality? What made me guardian over the longevity of another creature, one who could not communicate his thoughts on the matter?

But euthanasia was on all our minds, and the previous summer, when we went on vacation, I had for the first time left a note with the vet, indicating that if Baron became ill and in her opinion past healing, she had our permission to put him to sleep.

At Thanksgiving, when Dan came home from school, he expressed shock at Baron's decline.

"Can't you see he's suffering?" Dan cried. "Every movement hurts him. How can you let him live this way?"

"I don't know," I murmured, uncertain. "Maybe he's still getting enough out of life."

"To lie on a mat in the corner day and night?" Dan demanded. "Where's the life in that? Where's the dignity?"

I began talking to friends, abstractly at first, wondering how long we could avoid the decision, half hoping that the situation would resolve itself, that Baron would die gently in his sleep. Each morning when Lloyd and I went to wake the dogs, it was with the uneasy thought that Baron might not greet us.

As December came and the cold penetrated more deeply, the arguments pro and con weighed heavily on my mind. At last, I called the vet to come and give Baron a checkup.

She came, and I think I knew ahead of time what she would tell me. Lloyd, Shari, and I had discussed it the evening before. Lloyd was willing to abide by my judgment. Dan had already expressed his opinion. And Shari pleaded both sides with equal compassion.

The final decision was mine. It was I who had picked Baron as a puppy, just born, had phoned weekly to check on his progress until he was weaned, and had gone to bring him home in the car. It seemed appropriate that I be the one to resolve this last conflict.

After the vet examined Baron, she gave her prognosis. She could hear congestion in his chest, a harshness in his breathing. She felt several lumps in his abdomen. His hips, always weak, were sore to the touch. His bones protruded as muscle tissue broke down, and that cycle could not be reversed. His skin problems were obvious.

With no demands upon him, Baron could continue to live like this, more or less a captive of his infirmity, lying on the patio, perhaps taking pleasure in seeing us, in his food, and in his surroundings. But, with increasing rapidity, he would grow weaker. Inevitably, he would suffer cancer or heart disease or kidney failure. With the full onset of disease, he would have great discomfort and pain. How much pain, she could not judge. How long before its onset, she could not tell.

The vet gave me all the facts as she knew them. She gave me time to think. And she showed me both roads impartially.

Tomorrow, I told her, I wanted her to come again to the house, to let Baron lie on his own mat with me beside him, and then to give him the drug that would bring on his death. I did not want him to be taken away to a strange place, to be in fear. I wanted him to die at home, among his family. I would arrange ahead of time with the ASPCA to take the body. I wanted it to be tomorrow, so that we could have this one last day together, and so that we all could grow accustomed to the idea.

It was agreed. I made the arrangements. The vet was to arrive at ten, the ASPCA shortly afterward.

When I told Shari the plan, she elected to stay home from school until it was done. I agreed. It was her right to be with Baron, and I appreciated and respected her decision. She and I are very much alike. We would rather look the enemy straight in the face—if, indeed, death can be called an enemy. For Baron, I thought it was a gentle and loving release.

The date was December 9, 1976. And in the fullness of our emotions, Lloyd and I sought solace by writing our feelings on that day. We share them now as they were written then. Lloyd's letter said:

When I said goodbye to Baron this morning, I felt he was trying to tell me something. He tried to get up, but it hurt him. I don't know, if he could talk, whether he would say: Dad, I am tired of this life. Being in the patio is worse than being in jail. I can't run after balls. I hear noises but it is too painful for me to go to the gate. It hurts my lungs when I bark. It hurts to get up to get water. I can't get in the car anymore. I can't hold my bowels very well—sometimes I go at the front door. It is getting colder at night. I have nothing to look forward to but greater pain coupled with reduced activity and diminished dignity. I used to be "Baron de los Palos Colorados." I am now merely an old dog, full of sores, a feeble dog "de los Atrium."

Or would he say: Dad, don't let anyone hurt me. I love life, even though it pains me. Seeing my family, Jinxie and Jessica, even with my everyday pain is better than no existence at all. I look forward to my daily meal, barking at the gardener, and I like scaring the milkman, going for a ride and smelling new delights, and especially seeing Shari grow up. Often big Dan and Grandma come. (What ever happened to big Joe?) I trust you, Dad—you won't let anything happen to me. I only made one mistake—I let the power saw be stolen. I often think of the good old days—jumping for the ball in Moraga (but now my hip hurts from so much jumping), sleeping in the ivy, chasing cats, and playing baseball at the Historical Society picnic. Remember when I bit that goat? I'm sorry I pinned your friend against the wall during your poker game. When I came to Palos Verdes in that airplane, it was horrible. I told you then never again to leave me in the hands of strangers, and you said you wouldn't. I trust in you, Dad.

I wish I knew what Baron was trying to tell me.

My letter said:

Baron was born Sept. 9—eleven years ago.

In the night while I slept I thought about him—not

about the decision or my role, just about him. Last night we took him for his last walk. It was very crisp and cold and the moon was nearly round, like a big silver plate, seen between the leaves of our neighbor's gigantic eucalyptus trees. I wanted to show him the moon. I told him, "Look at the moon." But he kept his head down.

The children are more realistic than we. Shari made claim to his collar and tags. She spoke of keeping the body. It was not a good idea, I said. Dan had already said his goodbyes at Thanksgiving. Lloyd asked him, "Do you want us to wait till you come home and can say goodbye?" Dan said no. He felt we had waited too long already. It vindicated me.

I woke up glad to see the sun. I want him to have the sun. I think of this, his last morning. There is something very quiet and gentle and beautiful about *knowing*. There is sorrow, but also the control that comes from knowing that death will not be violent, that it will not force its way or intrude, that we are ready. In my heart I tell him, "Baron, dear dog, I give you the gift of gentle rest." As I look about, I am acutely conscious of every detail of this last day—as if it were my last day. I am suddenly struck with two powerful thoughts:

In a way, it is my last day too, for that part of me which experienced portions of life with him is also dying, except in memory. No longer will his presence make our past together a continuing chain of events. It is now irrevocably ended.

Also, I recognize that I have had these same "last day" feelings before. They combine sorrow with awe for the beauty of life and creation—it feels sad and heavy but right. We, mortal, are meant to know endings. They fit our souls. I felt endings when I went that very first day to school—babyhood died. I felt it too the day I left home for college, noticed the sun, the smell in the air, the exact feel of the worn tweed upholstery in the train that took me five hundred miles north. That day my childhood died. And when I became a bride, and when I became a mother, and when I gave up smoking, and when my father died, and when we left our beautiful town to follow a new opportunity—each time there was a last day, and each time I died. Each dying was needed for the next step, and each time I grew. I can only pray and marvel. Perhaps this day of the body's death is truly the prelude to another kind of living.

I have called the ASPCA again. I fear they may not come for hours, that Baron will lie too long, stiff and cold. I want his body to go quickly.

He went quickly. The vet was skillful and gentle. The drug was swift. The man from the ASPCA was prompt and very kind. A shot was administered to Baron as Shari and I sat holding him, and at that moment when his head rose up and he gave a long, last moan, I clutched Shari's hand very, very tightly.

140

We felt very close, we who had witnessed this dying. We felt close to one another and to the pulse of the world.

18

N o w i t i s summer again. The cats have passed
their first birthday. They have long since been "fixed,"
so our animal population won't explode. On Saturdays
I often see adorable puppies and kittens being given
away outside the supermarket, and I staunchly resist.
My three friends at home are enough, with their special
personalities, their individual ways of holding me captive.

Take Jinxie. She likes to watch TV. If I come
home late at night she reproaches me. At the sound of
my key, she scampers forth and sits straight before

me, head high, mouth tight. I pick her up. She gives a meow and a sorrowful blink. "I didn't get to see TV. I wanted to watch TV."

"But, Jinxie," I gently chide her, "you never really watch."

"Doesn't matter. Like to see TV. Like to sit with you."

"Ah, that's it, then. It's not so much the watching as the sitting on my lap for an hour or two, getting stroked gently behind the ears, with a little kiss now and then. That's it."

She handles Lloyd quite differently. Each morning when I set the table for breakfast, Jinx makes herself the centerpiece. Nose thrust forward, she makes passes at Lloyd's muffin. He brushes her aside. She retreats, gains momentum, and moves in on his cottage cheese.

"Get off, Jinxie!" we both yell.

She gazes at us astounded. "What? Off? Why would I get off when we're having breakfast here?"

Not long ago, Lloyd utterly lost patience and shouted at her in a tone so loud and harsh that she immediately leaped off the table and onto a chair. Her pupils contracted instantly and she sat stunned and motionless, her entire demeanor expressing such horror and pain that Lloyd and I stared at each other abashed. How could anyone have been so cruel?

The next day, and the next and the next, Jinxie

quietly resumed her center spot on the table, daintily sharing a tidbit of bacon, a speck of cheese, the crumbly end of an English muffin.

Jessica's wiles are different. Her attitude tells me she doesn't like to cuddle. Because she is tough, because she is Top Cat, I have to catch her as she streaks past. Then, as I place her in the crook of my arm, she throws back her head and puts her paw across my mouth, and, ever so gently, begins to knead and purr. I feel the little tickle of her claws on my lips. She stretches full length to my caress in sensual cat-contentment. In her fur I can smell the fresh scent of pine trees and eucalyptus.

At night, when Lloyd and I go out for our walk, we often hear a pitiful, resounding cry.

"It's Jessica," he says with a sigh. Back home again, he finds her in the patio or atop the roof.

"Yeow-oow!" she objects. "You're leaving, and I want to go inside. My food is there. What if you get killed—how will I ever get inside?"

Lloyd unlocks the door, puts her in. We resume our walk.

Sometimes, somehow, she sneaks out again. We get a block or two from home. We hear a rustling in the bushes, then faintly: "Mee-ow. Yow-yow."

"It's Jessica."

Heedless of passing autos, she throws herself gleefully at Lloyd's feet, and lies on her back doing the shimmy-shake routine until he picks her up. She begins at once to purr. "Ah, yes, carry me."

It is really ridiculous, Lloyd tells me, for a grown man to be seen carrying a kitty on his walk. I agree with him. We both agree we've been had.

At our house, we talk about our animals the way most parents talk about their kids. As soon as he's home from work, Lloyd wants a rundown.

"What did Barney do today?"

"Oh, he went after the paperboy. And I took him to the store."

"And what about Jinxie-Jessica?" (He always refers to them this way, as if they were one animal.)

"They slept a lot."

"Well, of course, they're tired. Especially Jessica. I heard her fighting last night, and she's got a scratch on her shoulder."

"I'll put on some salve."

Yes, they've taken over our conversation and our home, all but our bedroom. And even from there they must be forcibly evicted several times a week. Jinx capitulates instantly. But Jessica always hides under the bed, whence she must be prodded with a long stick and pulled out, claws digging frantically into the carpet.

My mother is amazed that cats and dogs can live

together at all without resultant mayhem. They manage as well as most human siblings, I explain, for all their disparity in physique. In their own way, the cats rule Barney, too. They have a hundred ways of sneaking past him to the high places he cannot reach, to the small places into which he cannot fit, to the forbidden places where he'd be spotted at once. Somehow they evoke his protective instincts. Could it be because he first found them?

I've seen the three of them lying on the living-room rug just a few inches apart. I think that in their hearts they'd all like to lie together like the proverbial lion and lambs, but, like all animals, they are realistic. The cats are well aware that at any moment Barney could revert to his primitive lust for the chase, and then they'd find themselves up a tree. So they keep their options open and their defenses up. They get along best when sleeping on opposite sides of the sliding glass door to the patio. With Barney out there on his rug and the cats inside on theirs, they can lie face to face, with the maximum of togetherness and the minimum of risk.

Outdoors, they have set up a sensible arrangement. Should the cats be caught running openly across the grass, they are fair game for a roundabout chase. But if they are lying peaceably in a chair or perched on the railings of the deck, Barney must offer them the courtesy and protection inherent in his status as watch-dog of the house.

Yes, he has risen to this task. He barks with proper ferocity at the gardener, holds the milkman in his accustomed terror, and makes a real display of teeth and ruff when a stranger comes to the gate. His defense of the car is truly impressive. He becomes just as hysterical as Baron ever did when I try to get gas.

Full grown, Barney is handsome and massive and (people tell me) formidable. But I know that in many ways he's still a kid at heart.

Take his relationship with water. Barney has never really gotten the fact that water pouring from the hose is fluid, unstable, and cannot be wrestled down to the ground like a fox or a bean bag. He persists in trying to catch the flow in his teeth, shaking his head, whirling, leaping, snapping, and getting doused in the snoot.

He has outgrown his penchant for digging. I reward him by keeping a good supply of fresh bones on hand. In the summer, he still pulls nectarines off the tree, but at least he eats them. In the fall, he eats the ripening apples.

Like a kid, he still loves vanilla ice-cream cones and going to the beach and playing ball—although he's never learned to share. If you want to play ball with Barney, you need two balls, one to throw as a diversion so he'll let you have the other one from his mouth.

Occasionally Barney sloughs off, ignores all his training, and reverts to acting like a spoiled brat. Then I remember Lois's motto: *"Own a pet, not a pest,"* and I take him out and put him through his paces again. It always helps to re-establish control. Even a short bit of rope attached to his collar symbolizes control and keeps him in line. I learned a lot from Lois. She taught me that one needn't put up with all sorts of irritating behavior in the misguided belief that dogs are just that way, and there's nothing you can do about it. I sometimes wish I'd taken her course earlier. It would have helped me with the kids.

Sometimes it's hard for me not to let disobedience slip by, partly because Barney's so much better now, partly because I'm a softie. Just last month, for instance, he ate my tennis hat, leaving only a few inches of brim. I'm not proud of it, but I ignored the incident. He must have taken a dislike to that tennis hat. I guess it didn't look good on me.

And sometimes he does weird things. Like the other night when we were all nicely sitting around the table, playing hearts. Barney suddenly jumped up and climbed into Lloyd's lap, nearly knocking him out in the attempt. Well, it wasn't really Barney's fault. He was provoked.

How was he provoked?

Well, Lloyd was whistling. He always whistles when he gets a good hand.

Lloyd insisted that he never whistles, certainly not when he gets a good hand. That would be a dead give-away.

He was whistling, and the whistling somehow incited Barney and made him try to climb up onto the table, whereupon he knocked over some glasses of soda pop and a bowl of nuts. I tried to ignore it, but it was too hilarious. Lloyd kept whistling innocently, and Barney kept on climbing.

Actually, the one who gets along best with Barney is Dan. When he comes home on vacations, the two of them run and romp as if they'd been pups together. And Dan talks to Barney. "Does the citizen want to go for a little ride in my car?" The two of them crowd into the front seat of Dan's tiny Alpine, another hilarious sight.

Barney is still too hyper to suit Shari. She complains that he tries to trip her on the stairs. (That's true. He does the same to me. It's quite a challenge to predict his attack and brace yourself accordingly.) He still accosts her girl friends. Especially when they're wearing shorts. And he insists on peeking into her bedroom when she's dressing. Gross dog.

I point out that you can't make a silk purse out of a sow's ear. I think Barney is a pretty good dog. For Barney.

Where Lloyd is concerned, I'm afraid the relationship has remained slightly strained. Lloyd likes a calm, dignified dog. A creature who, if he were human, would smoke a pipe and read the *Scientific Gazette*. And never engage in any extreme behavior.

Lloyd knows that conflicts and complaints upset me, so he follows the course of least resistance. If Barney happens to be lying in the hall, Lloyd makes a detour. If Barney is in the kitchen when Lloyd wants a snack, Lloyd decides to stick to his diet. When we walk with Barney, *I* hold the leash.

Lloyd issues few commands, and he holds slim expectations, being of the persuasion that dogs—like people—seldom really change, that they might temporarily mask their true inclinations, but a dummy is a dummy and a clown is a clown is a clown.

So we all made our adjustments and eased into a state of truce. Then came an amazing turn of events. Incredibly, Barney was going to become one of the main characters in a book titled *Reigning Cats and Dogs*.

The book was really going to be *published*.

A book about Barney? That dummy? That clown?

I said nothing: money talks.

From the moment that acceptance letter arrived, Lloyd looked at Barney and the cats with new eyes. Oh, stars, assets, contributors! Oh, promoters of family pride! Joy. Money. Fame.

I could see a different light in my husband's eyes as we sat at the table that night having dessert. Barney lay nervously at his feet, careful not to leap or paw or in any other way incur his master's displeasure.

We were talking about general matters. Suddenly Lloyd turned and looked Barney full in the face. Then he rose and went to the refrigerator, taking with him the remaining shell of his cantaloupe.

Barney tensed, alert to some unspoken command, like a psychic getting distant vibes. He quickly followed Lloyd to the refrigerator and sat down, straight, tall, expectant.

Lloyd opened the freezer door.

Barney's ears stood erect.

Lloyd took out a carton of vanilla ice cream. He brought it to the counter. He scooped out a generous portion and stuffed it into the cantaloupe shell. Then he bent down to Barney and waited while the dog licked out every last bit of the sweet treat.

I say that relationships *can* change. I'd say that a man must have a certain regard for a dog before he'll serve him cantaloupe à la mode.

Sonia Levitin, the author of many successful books for young people, lives in California with her family and their pets.